KANJI IDIOMS

MW00572674

KANJI
IDIOMS

•

George Wallace
&
Kayoko Kimiya

KODANSHA INTERNATIONAL
Tokyo • New York • London

Distributed in the United States by Kodansha America, Inc., 114 Fifth
Avenue, New York N.Y. 10011, and in the United Kingdom and continental
Europe by Kodansha Europe Ltd., 95 Aldwych, London WC2B 4JF.
Published by Kodansha International Ltd., 17-14 Otowa 1-chome, Bunkyo-ku,
Tokyo 112, and Kodansha America, Inc.

Contents

Preface

What are four-character compounds?
Why do we need to learn them?

When we were searching in the dark (*anchū-mosaku*), at a total loss what to call our book, we suddenly hit upon "A Guide to Japanese Four-Letter Words." Pithy, punchy, in your face. Unfortunately, also rather misleading. From *yoji-jukugo* to four-character compounds to four-letter words. Not a journey of a million miles, but our editors didn't see it that way. "What's wrong with a little harmless sheep's head but dog meat (*yōtō-kuniku*; false advertising)?" we asked, but it was like the east wind blowing into a horse's ear (*baji-tōfū*). They just didn't want to know.

So what are these *yoji-jukugo* (四字熟語)? Yoji-jukugo (or four-character compounds, as we often call them in this book) are words / expressions made up of four kanji joined together with no kana in between. Scholars might argue that bona fide yoji-jukugo are ones with a classical origin, but there seem to be no hard and fast rules on this point.

What we consider to be the real McCoy (*shōshin-shōmei*) yoji-jukugo is one that either (a) comprises two two-character compounds whose connection is not always clear at first sight (a three-day priest; a sheep's head but dog meat; a crisis, one hair), or (b) can only be understood if you have some background knowledge of the following fields: (i) Chinese history (the So song on four sides; the Go and the Etsu in the same boat; lying on firewood and licking liver), (ii) *kanbun* or classical Chinese (visit the past to know the new; as if there were no one around), (iii) Japanese history (a Japanese soul with Western learning), (iv) Japanese folk beliefs (a cold head and warm feet), and (v) Buddhist thought (a paradise death; entrusting one's life on one lotus leaf).

As you might have surmised by now, yoji-jukugo are cryptic, pithy, and somewhat arcane phrases. Use them correctly in your everyday conversation and you will blow your Japanese friends out of the water. Seeing the LDP climb into bed with their old foe, the Socialists, in a desperate attempt to hold onto power, all you need say is "It's the Go and the Etsu in the same boat, isn't it?" Your Japanese friends will be stunned that you have even heard of the Go and the Etsu, let alone know that they are synonymous for sworn enemies who by a trick of fate find themselves thrown together, having to cooperate with each other to survive.

Yoji-jukugo are handy not just for impressing your Japanese friends; they are also a useful way of saying a lot in a few words (thus minimizing the risk of your meaning going astray as you struggle with grammar and vocabulary problems). For example, when somebody manages to accomplish two goals at the same time by doing only one action, in English you can say they "killed two birds with one stone." In Japanese you say *isseki-nichō*; "one stone, two birds."

One other benefit you get when you use a four-character compound is that it will give your conversation the sort of patina bestowed upon English by the inclusion of words of Latin origin. It may sound snobbish, but it is a fact of life that the greater the number of Latinate words you use, the better your chances of commanding authority when you speak. "It's elementary, my dear Watson" has a certain something. "It's easy, my dear Watson" doesn't.

Just as English has borrowed much from Latin, so Japanese owes a great debt to Chinese. When you speak Japanese, you will create a much better impression if you sprinkle your conversation with kanji compounds, such as the ones included in this book. If you are in any doubt about this, please visit any Japanese bookstore and see the number of dictionaries dedicated wholly to the study and mastery of yoji-jukugo. University students are often tested on their knowledge of them at company interviews as a way of assessing not only their grasp of linguistic niceties but also their knowledge of centuries of classical wisdom.

A word of warning: with only four kanji in each expression, it is VITAL you get the pronunciation right; otherwise you will be greeted by those tiltings of the head and the polite smiles that we all know are the Japanese way of saying "Come again?"

Concerning the format of this book: each entry is first given in kanji with the romanized reading written alongside. Underneath there is first a literal translation (to convey as closely as possible the flavour of the Japanese original), then underneath that, a selection of more idiomatic English translations which hopefully make it clear when the expression can be used and when it cannot. To show how the yoji-jukugo can be used in a natural idiomatic way, we have written some sample sentences, one of which is as simple as possible, the other (or others) being slightly longer in length. In some cases where it was impossible to make a brief sample sentence of any validity, both sample sentences are of roughly the same length. Finally, we have added an English translation, which we hope brings out the flavour of the Japanese original. Entries are listed in the traditional Japanese a-i-u-e-o order.

We have also added some notes of linguistic and cultural interest. Though they tend to overlap, we have made an attempt to distinguish them by indicating the former with a ➡, and the latter by a ☐.

Some of the entries may strike you as being rather out-of-place in a book on yoji-jukugo (e.g., *man'in-densha* and *juken-jigoku*). A purist would not have included them as they do not belong to any of the categories mentioned earlier. "A packed commuter train is not inherently classical in origin, so why is it in the book?" you wonder. Because it (and the others) are (in our humble opinion) the continuation of the yoji-jukugo tradition, and if that sounds a load of baloney, then how about because you'll hear them in everyday Japanese speech and we reckoned you ought to know them.

We hope you enjoy dipping into this book and sprinkling its contents of Chinese and Buddhist knowledge and wisdom liberally throughout your daily conversation. To paraphrase the Roman poet Juvenal, this little book is a farrago of delights both ancient and modern. Enjoy!

はしがき

「四字熟語」は、中学以来勉強させられて、入社試験にまで出て、もういいよ、という方も多いのかも知れません。でも、そういう人も、「そりゃいいや、一石二鳥だ」とか、「羨ましいなあ、前途洋々で」とか、「もっと正々堂々とやれよ」とか、「有耶無耶にしないでほしいわね」などと、けっこう普段の会話の中で使っているはずです。四字熟語は、日本人同士の会話の中では、長々と説明することなく簡潔に、適切に、しかもちょっと洒落て、自分の言わんとするところを相手に印象づけて表現できる言い回しです。これほど便利な四字熟語ですが、英語を話したり書いたりするときには、直訳しても通じませんね。日本語だったらこういうときはあの四字熟語がピッタリなんだけど、と思って和英辞書を見ても、いまひとつしっくりこない。そんな経験はないでしょうか。

この本では、日常的に使う約200の四字熟語について、まずは直訳に近い意味、そして場合によっては説明が、次に様々な状況に応じて使い分けられる訳語が並んでいます。例文にあわせて読めば、どの日本語の表現が自分の言いたい内容にもっとも適切か、選ぶ際の参考になるはずです。

逆に、例文の英訳の方から読んでみるのもおもしろいと思います。"You've got to be careful" もいつも「注意しなければいけないよ」ではなくて「油断大敵だよ」と訳せるんだなど、英和辞典には出ていないけれど、そうかこの表現はこの四字熟語が使えるんだ、という発見があるのではないでしょうか。

この本に出てくる四字熟語は、昔からくり返し使われてきた、いわば古典的な表現が大部分となりますが、現代の生活が生み出した新しいものも多少加えられています。「学歴社会」、「単身赴任」、「植物人間」、「万国共通」などの熟語がそ

れにあたります。こうした表現は、はたして厳密に四字熟語と呼ぶかどうか意見のわかれるところでしょうが、ワープロをたたけば、ちゃんとセットになって現れるほど私たちの日常に密着しています。それだけに、日本語を学ぶ人、英語を学習する人の双方にとって大変参考になると考えとりあげました。この本を楽しく気軽に読んで、役に立てていただければ幸いです。

☰ Kanji Idioms ☰

曖昧模糊 *aimai-moko*
vague and indistinct
〜とした，〜としている vague, hazy, patchy, wishy-
washy

• そんな曖昧模糊とした説明で納得できると思ってるのかね。

*Sonna aimai-moko to shita setsumei de nattoku dekiru to omot-
te 'ru no ka ne.*

Do you really think you can convince me with such a wishy-
washy explanation?

• あいつの話は何だか曖昧模糊としていて、訳が分からなか
った よ。

*Aitsu no hanashi wa nandaka aimai-moko to shite ite, wake ga
wakaranakatta yo.*

The guy just went on and on in such a vague and roundabout
way that I had no idea what he was talking about.

• 僕にも確信があるわけじゃなくて、曖昧模糊とした印象に
過ぎないんだけどね。

*Boku ni mo kakushin ga aru wake ja nakute, aimai-moko to
shita inshō ni suginai n' da kedo ne.*

It is just a vague impression; it is not that I'm absolutely sure
about it.

➔ Synonymous expressions for 曖昧模糊とした are 曖昧な (*aimai na*)
and 漠然とした (*bakuzen to shita*).

青息吐息 *aoiki-toiki*

blue breath, exhaling breath (i.e., a sigh)

be in great distress, have a hard time of it

● 元金どころか利子を払うだけで青息吐息の毎日なんだ。

Gankin dokoro ka rishi o harau dake de aoiki-toiki no mai-nichi nan da.

Pay back the initial loan? You've got to be kidding! I'm busting a gut just trying to meet the interest payments.

● 早く人員を補充してくれなきゃ、こっちはもう青息吐息だよ。

Hayaku jin'in o hojū shite kurenakya, kotchi wa mō aoiki-toiki da yo.

They're gonna have to give us some extra staff soon; we're only just managing to keep our heads above water.

悪戦苦闘 *akusen-kutō*

a difficult battle, a bitter struggle

a long hard fight; ～する to fight desperately (with one's back to the wall, against heavy odds)

● 悪戦苦闘の末、明け方になってやっとレポートを書き終わったよ。

Akusen-kutō no sue, akegata ni natte yatto repōto o kakiowatta yo.

After a long hard slog I finally managed to finish my report by dawn.

● かれこれ半年も悪戦苦闘の連続だったけど、来月からは少し楽になりそうなんだ。

Karekore hantoshi mo akusen-kutō no mainichi datta kedo, raigetsu kara wa sukoshi raku ni narisō nan da.

For the past six months it's been nose to the grindstone all the way, but from next month it looks like things'll get easier.

● 忙しい日にバイトの子に休まれちゃって、朝から悪戦苦闘だよ。

Isogashii hi ni baito no ko ni yasumarechatte, asa kara akusen-kutō da yo.

We've been rushed off our feet all morning, thanks to that part-timer taking the day off just when we needed her most.

→ バイト (*baito*) is the shortened form of アルバイト (*arubaito*), meaning part-time job. It is a loan-word coming from the German word for work (Arbeit).

阿鼻叫喚 *abi-kyōkan*
screaming in hell
pandemonium, like a scene out of hell

● 戦闘の後の町は、まさに阿鼻叫喚の巷だった。

Sentō no ato no machi wa, masa ni abi-kyōkan no chimata datta.

After the battle the town looked like a scene from hell.

● 爆発事故で、工場は阿鼻叫喚の場となった。

Bakuhatsu-jiko de, kōjō wa abi-kyōkan no ba to natta.

After being hit by that explosion, the factory looked like something out of Dante's *Inferno*.

→ Originally 阿鼻 and 叫喚 are the names of two of the eight burning hells of Buddhism. In Sanskrit the two hells are called Avici and Raurava.

暗中模索 *anchū-mosaku*

searching in the dark

〜する to grope blindly in the dark, to be (all) at sea,
to be at a (total) loss

• どこから始めたらいいのか、まだ暗中模索だよ。

Doko kara hajimetara ii no ka, mada anchū-mosaku da yo.

I'm still totally in the dark as to where to begin.

• 大変なのは分かるが、いつまでも暗中模索の状態が続いて
るのはちょっと困るな。

*Taihen na no wa wakaru ga, itsu made mo anchū-mosaku no
jōtai ga tsuzuite 'ru no wa chotto komaru na.*

I realize things are difficult, but your continued cluelessness is
not making our life any easier.

• 暗中模索しているうちに、ふっと良い考えがひらめいたん
だ。

*Anchū-mosaku shite iru uchi ni, futto yoi kangae ga hirameita
n' da.*

There I was, wondering what on earth I should do when suddenly I had a great idea.

意気消沈 *iki-shōchin*

spirits sinking

with a heavy heart, with a sinking heart; 〜する to be
depressed (dejected, discouraged, downhearted), to be
down in the dumps, to have the mopes (the blues), to
feel like you have had all the wind knocked out of you

• 滑り止めの大学に落ちてから、すっかり意気消沈してしま
ってるんだよ。

*Suberidome no daigaku ni ochite kara, sukkari iki-shōchin shite
shimatte 'ru n' da yo.*

Not getting into that university really bummed me out; it was
my fail-safe choice.

❑ 滑り止めの大学 (*suberidome no daigaku*): In Japan students
usually apply to about half a dozen different universities. The
university they most want to enter is referred to as their 第1志
望校 (*daiichi shibō-kō*; their first-choice); their second-choice
is 第2志望校 (*daini shibō-kō*), their third 第3志望校 (*daisan
shibō-kō*), ad infinitum. Just in case they fail the entrance
exams to all their principal choices, most high school students
sit the exam for a less academically-challenging university. In
colloquial Japanese 滑る (*suberu*; to slip, slide) is a euphemism
for failing an exam. When you fail your first-to-nth-choices,
your *suberidome* is the university where you put a stop to your
"slide."

• そんなに意気消沈することないよ。君のせいじゃないんだ
から。

*Sonna ni iki-shōchin suru koto nai yo. Kimi no sei ja nai n' da
kara.*

Don't let it get you down. After all, it wasn't your fault.

➜ If you are looking for a phrase with the opposite meaning, use 意気
揚々 (*iki-yōyō*).

意気投合 *iki-tōgō*
spirits joining (spirits fusing)
mutual understanding, affinity, sympathy; 〜する to
be like-minded, to find a kindred spirit, to get on like a
house on fire, to be on the same wavelength, to speak
the same language, to hit it off with someone, to see
eye to eye with someone

• 寿司屋のカウンターで隣合った人と意気投合しちゃってね。

Sushiya no kauntā de tonariatta hito to iki-tōgō shichatte ne.

I really hit it off with this guy who was sitting next to me at the sushi bar.

• 鈴木さんとはすっかり意気投合して、家族ぐるみのつき合いをしていますよ。

Suzuki-san to wa sukkari iki-tōgō shite, kazoku-gurumi no tsukiai o shite imasu yo.

Ol' Suzuki and me, we're great buddies, always inviting each other's family around.

意気揚々 *iki-yōyō*

spirits soaring

triumphant(ly), exultant(ly), elated(ly), in triumph, in high spirits; 〜と、〜とする to be in good cheer, to be in a buoyant mood, to be over the moon, to be cock-a-hoop, to be as pleased as Punch

---

• 大口の契約がとれたって、意気揚々と報告して来たよ。

Ōguchi no keiyaku ga toreta tte, iki-yōyō to hōkoku shite kita yo.

He's just told me about that big new contract he pulled. He was practically walking on air.

• 合格発表を見に行った娘が、意気揚々としてもどって来た。

Gōkaku-happyō o mi ni itta musume ga, iki-yōyō to shite modotte kita.

My daughter went to check out her exam results and came back on cloud nine.

→ A synonymous expression is 意気軒昂 (*iki-kenkō*).

• 社長は「この製品は絶対売れる」と意気軒昂だ。

Shachō wa "Kono seihin wa zettai ureru" to iki-kenkō da.

The boss is all fired up about the product, saying it is sure to sell.

異口同音 *iku-dōon*

(from) different mouths (come) the same sound

〜 に with one voice, by common consent, unanimously, as one, all of one accord

---

• 葬儀の参列者は、異口同音に彼の人柄のよさを口にした。

Sōgi no sanretsu-sha wa, iku-dōon ni kare no hitogara no yosa o kuchi ni shita.

All the mourners at the funeral were unanimous in their praise of his good character.

• 「ビートルズのようなすぐれたバンドは、もう二度と現れないだろう」と音楽ファンは異口同音に言う。

"Bītoruzu no yō na sugureta bando wa, mō nido to arawarenai darō" to ongaku-fan wa iku-dōon ni iu.

All music buffs are agreed: there will never be another band quite like the Beatles.

• 同僚は異口同音に今辞表を出したら損だと忠告してくれた。

Dōryō wa iku-dōon ni ima jihyō o dashitara son da to chūkoku shite kureta.

All my colleagues without exception advised me against handing in my resignation now.

→ Care should be taken when writing this four-letter compound. Japanese schoolchildren often mistakenly write it as 異句同音. Other expressions meaning "unanimously" include 口を揃えて (*kuchi o soroete*) and 口々に (*kuchiguchi ni*). When various people use exactly the same words, you can use either 異口同音 or 口を揃えて, but not 口々に, as this is used when people say similar things (but each person uses a slightly different expression).

意識不明 *ishiki-fumei*

consciousness unclear

unconscious, senseless

- 倒れてしばらくは意識不明で、このまま駄目になるんじゃないかと思われたそうだ。

Taorete shibaraku wa ishiki-fumei de, kono mama dame ni naru n' ja nai ka to omowareta sō da.

I was unconscious for some time after I collapsed, and apparently they thought that might be the end of me.

- 事故に会った人は3人で、そのうち1人は意識不明の重体です。

Jiko ni atta hito wa sannin de, sono uchi hitori wa ishiki-fumei no jūtai desu.

Of the three people involved in the accident, one of them is unconscious and in serious condition.

以心伝心 *ishin-denshin*

from one heart to another

immediate communication from one mind to another, telepathy, telepathic communication between people, tacit understanding, intuitively shared thoughts or feelings, to be able to read each other's mind

- これ以上言わせるなよ、以心伝心だろう。

Kore ijō iwaseru na yo, ishin-denshin darō.

Don't make me spell it out. You must know what I'm getting at, surely.

- 父の気持ちは以心伝心でよく分かった。

Chichi no kimochi wa ishin-denshin de yoku wakatta.

Dad didn't have to say a word. I knew exactly what he was thinking.

● 俺とあいつは以心伝心の間柄なんだ。

Ore to aitsu wa ishin-denshin no aidagara nan da.

He and I know each other so well that we can tell what the other's thinking.

一期一会 *ichigo-ichie*
in one lifetime, one meeting
a once-in-a-lifetime meeting

● この歳になると、どの出会いも一期一会と思って大切にしていますよ。

Kono toshi ni naru to, dono deai mo ichigo-ichie to omotte taisetsu ni shite imasu yo.

When you get to be my age, every time you meet someone you think of it as a unique opportunity and make the most of it.

● 一期一会と思えば、人と言い争う気持ちもなくなりますね。

Ichigo-ichie to omoeba, hito to iiarasou kimochi mo nakunari-masu ne.

When you think of each and every moment as precious, you don't feel like getting involved in arguments with people.

❏ Originally part of the teaching of the tea ceremony: every occasion of extending hospitality to another person is a particular opportunity never to recur in one's lifetime, so one should try to make the occasion perfect.

一日千秋 *ichijitsu-senshū*

one day (is like) a thousand autumns

to look forward to something eagerly; 〜 の 思 い to wait impatiently for something (and while you wait, time seems to tick by so slowly that one day seems to last forever)

● 一日千秋の思いで、この日を待っていました。

Ichijitsu-senshū no omoi de, kono hi o matte imashita.

I feel as though I have been waiting for this day forever.

● 結果が発表されるまでの１週間は、一日千秋の思いだったよ。

Kekka ga happyō sareru made no isshūkan wa, ichijitsu-senshū no omoi datta yo.

The week I spent waiting for my results to come out was one of the longest of my life.

一念発起 *ichinen-hokki*

arouse the single mind

〜する to make up one's mind (to do something)

● リストラで会社に居づらくなったよ、一念発起して脱サラするかな。

Risutora de kaisha ni izuraku natta yo, ichinen-hokki shite datsu-sara suru ka na.

What with the restructuring, life at the office isn't getting any easier. Maybe I'll just take the plunge and strike out on my own.

❏ 脱サラ (*datsusara*) is a compound of 脱 (escaping) and サラ, a shortened form of サラリーマン (company employee). Together they refer to the ever-increasing phenomenon of disgruntled white-collar workers who quit their companies and the rat-race (usually to do something slightly "alternative," such as open a bar, become a musician, or free-lance).

● これからしばらくはマイホームの買い時だと聞いて一念発起したらしく急に貯金を始めた。

Kore kara shibaraku wa maihōmu no kaidoki da to kiite ichinen-hokki shita rashiku kyū ni chokin o hajimeta.

He heard that now's a good time to buy, so apparently he immediately started saving up for his own home.

❑ Owning one's own home is the dream of many Japanese, especially those living in or around Tokyo and Osaka, where land prices are still so astronomical that a detached house on a tiny plot of land is about as affordable as a mansion in Manhattan or a palatial penthouse in Paris.

一部始終 *ichibu-shijū*

the whole thing from beginning to end (from start to finish)

the full particulars, all the details, the whole story (from beginning to end), the complete run-down from A to Z, all the ins and outs

---

● 犯行の一部始終が、防犯ビデオに録画されていた。

Hankō no ichibu-shijū ga, bōhan-bideo ni rokuga sarete ita.

The security cameras recorded the whole scene on video, from beginning to end.

● 少年は犯行の一部始終を見ていた。

Shōnen wa hankō no ichibu-shijū o mite ita.

The boy watched as the crime unfolded before his very eyes.

● 一部始終が分かって、やっと納得したよ。

Ichibu-shijū ga wakatte, yatto nattoku shita yo.

Now that I know the whole story, I'm perfectly happy with the situation.

一網打尽 *ichimō-dajin*

with one (throw of the) net, catch the lot

a wholesale arrest; 〜 にする to catch, to arrest the whole gang in one go (in one big raid, in one big round-up, in one fell swoop)

• これで麻薬密売組織は一網打尽だ。

Kore de mayaku-mitsubai-soshiki wa ichimō-dajin da.

With this raid we'll catch the whole drug smuggling ring in one fell swoop.

• 暴走族を一網打尽にするため　特別班が出動した。

Bōsō-zoku o ichimō-dajin ni suru tame, tokubetsu-han ga shutsudō shita.

Special police units were mobilized in the raid to round up the motorbike gangs.

• 集団スリは、刑事たちに一網打尽にされた。

Shūdan-suri wa, keiji-tachi ni ichimō-dajin ni sareta.

The team of pickpockets was rounded up as the detectives closed in.

一目瞭然 *ichimoku-ryōzen*

clear at a glance

clearly, obviously, as clear as day(light), evidently, plain to see, obvious, you could tell right away that …

• ここが長い間空き家だったのは一目瞭然だな。

Koko ga nagai aida akiya datta no wa ichimoku-ryōzen da na.

It's plain to see that this house has been empty for a long time.

● 彼がもう相当飲んでるのは一目瞭然よ。

Kare ga mō sōtō nonde 'ru no wa ichimoku-ryōzen yo.

You don't have to be Sherlock Holmes to see he's had a few drinks already.

● 何が起こったかは一目瞭然だった。

Nani ga okotta ka wa ichimoku-ryōzen datta.

It was patently obvious what had happened.

● こんな一目瞭然の間違いを見逃すなんて、たるんでるんじゃないか。

Konna ichimoku-ryōzen no machigai o minogasu nante, tarunde 'ru n' ja nai ka.

To miss such a glaring mistake really beggars belief. Get a grip, man!

一蓮托生 *ichiren-takushō*
on the same lotus leaf, trust one's life (with the others')
being born on the same lotus leaf in Buddhist heaven;
casting one's lot with another; being in the same boat;
thrown together by a quirk of fate; facing the same fate

● 俺たちは一蓮托生だ。自分だけ逃げようったって、そうは行かないぞ。

Ore-tachi wa ichiren-takushō da. Jibun dake nigeyō 'tta tte, sō wa ikanai zo.

We're in this together. If you're thinking of making a run for it by yourself, buddy, just think again.

● 密告するのは勝手だけど、あんたも一蓮托生で刑務所行きだぜ。

Mikkoku suru no wa katte da kedo, anta mo ichiren-takushō de keimusho-yuki da ze.

Go on then, squeal on me. See what good it does you. We're in this together, and we'll both end up going to jail.

● 与党と野党は、結局一蓮托生だったわけだ。

Yotō to yatō wa, kekkyoku ichiren-takushō datta wake da.

So, it turns out the ruling and opposition parties were working in cahoots.

❏ Originally this expression came from Buddhism and referred to the belief that people who loved each other in this world would be joyfully reunited in paradise, spending eternity together on a lotus leaf. Now the expression has come to take on a radically different meaning and is used in situations when people are thrown together and find themselves in dire straits.

一攫千金 *ikkaku-senkin*
(with) one grab (get) a thousand (pieces of) gold
making a fortune at a stroke, a bonanza; to get rich quick, to strike oil; to strike it rich, to hit the jackpot, to make a killing

---

● 一攫千金を夢見て、馬券を買うときはいつも大穴を狙ってる。

Ikkaku-senkin o yumemite, baken o kau toki wa itsumo ōana o neratte 'ru.

He's always putting his money on the horses, going for the big win that'll make him an overnight millionaire.

● 一攫千金を狙うことばかり考えないで、地道に働きなさい。

Ikkaku-senkin o nerau koto bakari kangaenai de, jimichi ni hatarakinasai.

Instead of dreaming up ways of getting rich quick, why don't you try doing some honest work for a change?

● 毎年ジャンボ宝くじを買ってるけど、まだ一攫千金の夢は夢のままだよ。

Maitoshi janbo-takarakuji o katte 'ru kedo, mada ikkaku-senkin no yume wa yume no mama da yo.

Every year I buy tickets for the grand slam lottery, but my dreams of hitting the jackpot have yet to come true.

● バブルの崩壊以後、一攫千金の儲け話はなくなった。

Baburu no hōkai igo, ikkaku-senkin no mōkebanashi wa naku-natta.

Since the bubble economy burst, you don't hear so much talk of people getting rich overnight.

➡ The correct way to write this expression is 一攫千金 but it can also be written 一獲千金. In either case the pronunciation is the same. A synonymous expression is 濡れ手で粟 (*nurete de awa*), which literally translated means "(to grasp) millet grain with wet hands."

一家団欒 *ikka-danran*
one family all together
the whole family happily united, a happy home, a happy family

---

● 子供たちが大きくなって、昔のような一家団欒の時間が少なくなったよ。

Kodomo-tachi ga ōkiku natte, mukashi no yō na ikka-danran no jikan ga sukunaku natta yo.

Since the kids have grown up, we don't seem to spend as much time together as we used to.

● 一家団欒といっても、家じゃみんながテレビの方を見ていてあまり話はしないんだ。

Ikka-danran to itte mo, uchi ja minna ga terebi no hō o mite ite amari hanashi wa shinai n' da.

I wouldn't say we're one big happy family. There's not much talking, what with everybody staring at the TV.

一喜一憂 *ikki-ichiyū*
one joy, one sadness
〜する to alternate between hope and despair; to be up
in the clouds one minute, down in the dumps the next;
to be on an emotional rollercoaster; to swing from joy
to sorrow

• その程度のことで、一喜一憂するんじゃない。

Sono teido no koto de, ikki-ichiyū suru n' ja nai.

Don't get worked up over a little thing like that.

• 試合は接戦で、点が入る度にそれぞれのチームの応援団が
一喜一憂している。

*Shiai wa sessen de, ten ga hairu tabi ni sorezore no chīmu no
ōendan ga ikki-ichiyū shite iru.*

It was a close game and each time somebody scored, the cheer
leaders went into ecstasies of pleasure or pain.

• たいして貯金があるわけじゃないのに、利率が変わるたび
に一喜一憂してしまうんです。

*Taishite chokin ga aru wake ja nai no ni, riritsu ga kawaru
tabi ni ikki-ichiyū shite shimau n' desu.*

I haven't got much in the way of savings but even so, every
change in the interest rates has me either jumping for joy or
ready to jump off a cliff.

一挙一動 *ikkyo-ichidō*
one gesture and one move
every move one makes

• 彼女の一挙一動は絵になってるじゃないか。

Kanojo no ikkyo-ichidō wa e ni natte 'ru ja nai ka.

She looks the part no matter what she does.

● 有名な人になると、一挙一動に注目されて不自由でしょうね。

Yūmei na hito ni naru to, ikkyo-ichidō ni chūmoku sarete fu-jiyū deshō ne.

Once you become famous, every little move you make is under the spotlight; it must be a strain.

● 一挙一動まで監視されてるみたいで嫌だよ。

Ikkyo-ichidō made kanshi sarete 'ru mitai de iya da yo.

It's horrible. I feel like I'm being watched whatever I do.

一件落着 *ikken-rakuchaku*
one matter settled and done
the matter has been settled; it's all done and dusted

● 何カ月にも渡った捜査が実って、事件は一件落着した。

Nankagetsu ni mo watatta sōsa ga minotte, jiken wa ikken-rakuchaku shita.

After an investigation that lasted many months, the case was successfully concluded.

● これでやっと一件落着したと思ったのに、また横槍が入ったんだって？

Kore de yatto ikken-rakuchaku shita to omotta no ni, mata yokoyari ga haitta n' datte?

Just when I thought it was all over, now you tell me someone else is meddling in the matter?

❏ There is a long-running Japanese TV drama called *Tōyama no Kin-san* (遠山の金さん), which is set in feudal times. At the end of every episode the hero, Kin-san (a young judge), always brings the villains to book uttering his weekly punchline of *ikken-rakuchaku* ("That sews up another case for this week, boys.")

一生懸命 *isshō-kenmei*

one lifetime laying down one's life

with all one's might, (try) as hard as one can, with all one's heart and soul, putting all one's energy into

---

• もっと一生懸命やりなさい。

Motto isshō-kenmei yarinasai.

Come on! You can do better than that!

• どんなに一生懸命に勉強しても、おれはどうせ頭が悪いんだからだめなんだよ。

Donna ni isshō-kenmei ni benkyō shite mo, ore wa dōse atama ga warui n' da kara dame nan da yo.

No matter how hard I study, I'm never going to make it 'cause I just don't have the brains.

➜ Originally written 一所懸命 with the character for "place." This dates from the time in feudal Japan when a samurai would lay down his life to defend his territory.

一触即発 *isshoku-sokuhatsu*

one touch, immediate explosion

a touch-and-go situation, a potentially explosive situation, a volatile situation, sitting on a powder keg

---

• 政府軍とゲリラの間の緊張が高まり、一触即発の状態にある。

Seifu-gun to gerira no aida no kinchō ga takamari, isshoku-sokuhatsu no jōtai ni aru.

The tension between the government troops and the guerilla forces has reached such a pitch that the situation could blow up at any moment.

• 隣のご夫婦は普段から喧嘩が絶えず、一触即発の関係だ。

Tonari no gofūfu wa fudan kara kenka ga taezu, isshoku-sokuhatsu no kankei da.

The couple next-door do nothing but quarrel, the least thing setting them off.

• 大物政治家の突然の逮捕で、永田町は一触即発の緊張感に包まれた。

Ōmono seiji-ka no totsuzen no taiho de, Nagatachō wa isshoku-sokuhatsu no kinchō-kan ni tsutsumareta.

With the sudden arrest of a high-ranking politician, the whole government was thrown into an volatile state of high tension.

❏ 永田町 (Nagatachō) is the area in central Tokyo where the Diet and the Prime Minister's residence are located. Just as in England we often say Whitehall when we mean the British government (likewise Americans often say Capitol Hill), in Japan they often use Nagatachō to refer to the Diet and/or the government.

一進一退 *isshin-ittai*
one forward, one back
ebb and flow, back and forth, ding-dong, see-saw; two steps forward, two steps back

---

• 父の病状は一進一退で、楽観は出来ないそうだ。

Chichi no byōjō wa isshin-ittai de, rakkan wa dekinai sō da.

Some days Dad's condition gets better, some days worse. There isn't a lot of room for optimism, I'm told.

• 政府間交渉は一進一退を繰り返している。

Seifu-kan kōshō wa isshin-ittai o kurikaeshite iru.

The governments' negotiations are an endless repetition of two steps forward, two steps back.

一心同体 *isshin-dōtai*

one heart, the same body
of one heart and mind, as one mind and body

• 「夫婦は一心同体」というのは幻想じゃないでしょうか。

"Fūfu wa isshin-dōtai" to iu no wa gensō ja nai deshō ka.

When they say man and wife are of one heart and mind, isn't that just a fantasy (illusion)?

• おまえと俺とは一心同体なんだから、何でも打ち明けてくれよ。

Omae to ore to wa isshin-dōtai nan da kara, nan de mo uchi-akete kure yo.

We're one and the same, you and me. You can tell me anything.

一世一代 *isse-ichidai*

one generation, one lifetime
once in a lifetime

• 今回の独立開業は、僕にとっては一世一代の大ばくちなんですよ。

Konkai no dokuritsu-kaigyō wa, boku ni totte wa isse-ichidai no ōbakuchi nan desu yo.

I'm taking the chance of my life starting up this new business on my own.

• 一世一代の決断をして、衆議院選挙に出ることにしました。

Isse-ichidai no ketsudan o shite, shūgi-in senkyo ni deru koto ni shimashita.

Taking what might be the most important decision of my life, I've decided to run as a candidate in the parliamentary elections (for the House of Representatives).

一石二鳥 *isseki-nichō*

one stone, two birds
to kill two birds with one stone

• そうしてもらえると、一石二鳥でこちらも助かりますよ。

Sō shite moraeru to, isseki-nichō de kochira mo tasukarimasu yo.

If you would do that, we could kill two birds with one stone, which would be a big help to me.

• 一石二鳥どころか、一石三鳥をねらった欲張りな案なんです。

Isseki-nichō dokoro ka, isseki-sanchō o neratta yokubari na an nan desu.

Isn't this idea great? We're aiming not to kill two birds with the one stone, but three!

➡ A synonymous expression to this is 一挙両得 (*ikkyo-ryōtoku*). Of the two expressions, 一石二鳥 is by far the more commonly used.

一朝一夕 *itchō-isseki*

one morning, one evening
in a day, overnight, in a short time, in the twinkling of an eye

---

• 人は一朝一夕に変わるものじゃないから、長い目で見てやろう。

Hito wa itchō-isseki ni kawaru mono ja nai kara, nagai me de mite yarō.

People don't change overnight. We've gotta be patient on this one.

• そういう問題は、一朝一夕には解決しないよ。

Sō iu mondai wa, itchō-isseki ni wa kaiketsu shinai yo.

This isn't the sort of problem that can be solved overnight, you know.

➡ This expression is always followed by a negative clause. Thus you cannot say 一朝一夕に～する. The correct usage is 一朝一夕には～しない／出来ない.

一長一短 *itchō-ittan*

one long, one short

having both merits and demerits, both good points and bad points, both pros and cons

---

• 応募者は結構集まったが、どの人も一長一短だね。

Ōbo-sha wa kekkō atsumatta ga, dono hito mo itchō-ittan da ne.

We've had quite a lot of applicants, but they are all much of a muchness.

• どちらの案にも一長一短があって、決めかねているんだよ。

Dochira no an ni mo itchō-ittan ga atte, kimekanete iru n' da yo.

Both proposals have their good and bad points, which makes choosing between them difficult (so I can't make up my mind).

➡ This expression is used when comparing two or more items, all of which have their good points and their bad points. You cannot use it when simply talking about one thing. Thus you can't say あの人には一長一短がある to mean "He has good points and bad points." However, it's okay to say あの人を採用した場合には一長一短がある, because in this situation you are comparing two alternatives—whether to hire him or not—and talking about the pros and cons of each.

一刀両断 *ittō-ryōdan*

cut in half (in two) with one sword

〜する to take a drastic step or measure, to solve a problem once and for all, to cut the Gordian knot, to deal with a matter decisively, to strike at the heart of the matter

---

- 「責任は相手にある」と一刀両断のもとに言い放った。

"Sekinin wa aite ni aru" to ittō-ryōdan no moto ni iihanatta.

He took the situation by the scruff of its neck and laid the blame clearly at the other guy's feet.

- 我々の販売促進策は、まだ生温いと社長に一刀両断された。

Wareware no hanbai-sokushin-saku wa, mada namanurui to shachō ni ittō-ryōdan sareta.

The boss really laid it on the line (put the knife in) when he told us our ideas for increasing sales were half-baked.

一発勝負 *ippatsu-shōbu*

one shot decides who wins

go for broke; all or nothing

- 最後のレースでは、一発勝負で大穴をねらった。

Saigo no rēsu de wa, ippatsu-shōbu de ōana o neratta.

In the last race I went all out for the big win.

- これ以上交渉を続けても拉致があかないよ。そろそろ一発勝負に出た方がいい。

Kore ijō kōshō o tsuzukete mo rachi ga akanai yo. Sorosoro ippatsu-shōbu ni deta hō ga ii.

There's no point continuing any further with the negotiations—we're getting nowhere. We'd better go for broke.

一般公開 *ippan-kōkai*
general opening
open to the public; on general release

- あの寺の宝物は普段は一般公開されていないから、今がチャンスだよ。

Ano tera no hōmotsu wa fudan wa ippan-kōkai sarete inai kara, ima ga chansu da yo.

That temple's sacred treasures aren't usually open to the public, so now's your chance to see them.

- 僕は、一般公開の前のプレヴューで見たんだけど、評判通りいい映画だったね。

Boku wa, ippan-kōkai no mae no purevū de mita n' da kedo, hyōban-dōri ii eiga datta ne.

I saw the film at a preview before it went on general release. It was as good as it's cracked up to be.

一歩手前 *ippo-temae*
one step before
one step short of, on the verge of, (barely) inches away from

---

- 彼女とは婚約する一歩手前まで行ってたんだが、些細なことから喧嘩別れしてそのままになってしまったんだ。

Kanojo to wa kon'yaku suru ippo-temae made itte 'ta n' da ga, sasai na koto kara kenka-wakare shite sono mama ni natte shimatta n' da.

We were on the verge of getting engaged when we had a row over something petty and split up, and that's the way things have stayed.

- 受話器を置いてハッと気がついたら、もう火事の一歩手前

でした。それ以来、天ぷらを揚げてるときは電話に出ない
ことにしてるんです。

Juwa-ki o oite hatto ki ga tsuitara, mō kaji no ippo-temae deshita. Sore irai, tenpura o agete 'ru toki wa denwa ni denai koto ni shite 'ru n' desu.

Just as I hung up, I was surprised to find that I almost had a fire on my hands. Since then, I've made it a practice never to answer the phone while deep-frying tempura.

意味深長 *imi-shinchō*

meaning, deep and long

very meaningful, of profound significance, fraught (pregnant) with meaning, speaking volumes

---

• 彼がさっき言ったことは、意味深長だよ。

Kare ga sakki itta koto wa, imi-shinchō da yo.

What he just said is of great significance. / What he said a moment ago really ought to be listened to.

• ずいぶんと意味深長な発言だったね。

Zuibun to imi-shinchō na hatsugen datta ne.

That was a very profound comment, wasn't it? / You really hit the hammer on the nail with what you said back then, didn't you?

• 彼は意味深長な笑いを浮かべて彼女の話を聞いていた。

Kare wa imi-shinchō na warai o ukabete kanojo no hanashi o kiite ita.

He listened to what she was saying with a smile on his lips that spoke volumes (with a meaningful smile on his lips).

→ In colloquial Japanese it is very common to abbreviate this four-character compound and simply say (or write) イミシン (*imishin*).

• 彼の発言、ずいぶんイミシンじゃないか。

Kare no hatsugen, zuibun imishin ja nai ka.

I'd say there was something behind what he said, wouldn't you?

● イミシンな返事だったなあ。なんかワケアリだぜ。

Imishin na henji datta nā. Nanka wakeari da ze.

There was more to that answer than met the eye. He must be up to something.

慇懃無礼 *ingin-burei*

politely insolent

feigned politeness, being overpolite, being ever so polite

● あの人の慇懃無礼な言い方が、嫌で嫌で仕方がないんだ。

Ano hito no ingin-burei na iikata ga, iya de iya de shikata ga nai n' da.

I really can't stand his way of talking. He's so fawningly polite it makes me sick.

● 前もって連絡しなかったこちらも悪かったけれど、先方の断り方は実に慇懃無礼だった。

Mae-motte renraku shinakatta kochira mo warukatta keredo, senpō no kotowarikata wa jitsu ni ingin-burei datta.

I was at fault for not making contact beforehand, but the way they turned me away was absolutely the worst kind of insincere politeness.

右往左往 *uō-saō*

going right and going left

〜する to run about in utter confusion, to run pell-mell, to rush about like a headless chicken, to lose one's head, to get into a panic

- こんなことでいちいち右往左往するなんて、みっともないよ。

Konna koto de ichiichi uō-saō suru nante, mittomo nai yo.

To let yourself get worked up over something like this really makes you look bad.

- 幹事の連絡の不行き届きで、みんなが右往左往させられてしまった。

Kanji no renraku no fu-yukitodoki de, minna ga uō-saō sase-rarete shimatta.

Because the (party's, meeting's) organizer was careless about notifying people, there was a lot of needless running around.

有象無象 *uzō-muzō*
with form, without form
the rabble; the riffraff; every Tom, Dick and Harry; everyone and his brother

---

- 有象無象の自称「宮沢賢治研究家」がいるけど、本当に深く勉強している人は少ない。

Uzō-muzō no jishō "Miyazawa Kenji kenkyū-ka" ga iru kedo, hontō ni fukaku benkyō shite iru hito wa sukunai.

There are legions of self-proclaimed scholars of Miyazawa Kenji, but very few are really doing serious research.

❏ 宮沢賢治 Miyazawa Kenji (1896-1933) was a famous Japanese poet and writer of children's stories.

- 有名人の周りには、有象無象の人たちが金魚の糞のようについてくるものだ。

Yūmei-jin no mawari ni wa, uzō-muzō no hitotachi ga kingyo no fun no yō ni tsuite kuru mono da.

Famous people attract all kinds of riffraff like flies.

❑ 金魚の糞 (*kingyo no fun*; goldfish droppings): In this vivid and common figure of speech, the droppings of the goldfish, which tend to trail after the fish until becoming detached, are likened to human hangers-on.

海千山千 *umisen-yamasen*

a thousand (years) in the sea and a thousand (years) in the mountains

a sly old dog, a crafty old fox

• 彼女おとなしそうにしてたけど、結構海千山千だぜ。

Kanojo otonashisō ni shite 'ta kedo, kekkō umisen-yamasen da ze.

She acted all shy and quiet, but she ain't nobody's fool.

• 私のような海千山千の女は、これぐらいのことじゃ驚きませんよ。

Watashi no yō na umisen-yamasen no onna wa, kore gurai no koto ja odorokimasen yo.

Don't think you're gonna shock a woman like me with something like that.

• 先方は海千山千の強者だから、気をつけろよ。

Senpō wa umisen-yamasen no tsuwamono da kara, ki o tsukero yo.

The other guy's crafty as a fox and a real go-getter, so watch your step.

• あの海千山千がそんな脅しぐらいでびびるもんか。

Ano umisen-yamasen ga sonna odoshi gurai de bibiru mon ka.

Do you really think a threat like that's going to make him quake in his boots? He's seen it all before.

❑ This four-character compound has its origins in the folk belief that a snake will turn into a dragon after living a thousand years in the sea and a thousand years in the mountains.

有耶無耶 *uya-muya*

to be, not to be

vague, unclear, fuzzy; 〜になる to be left up in the air, unresolved, vague; 〜にする to leave (something) up in the air, unresolved, vague

---

• 戦後の混乱の中で、事件の真相は有耶無耶になってしまった。

Sengo no konran no naka de, jiken no shinsō wa uya-muya ni natte shimatta.

In the midst of all the post-war confusion it became impossible to tell what the truth of the incident was.

• これは大事なことなんだから、有耶無耶にしないでください よ。

Kore wa daiji na koto nan da kara, uya-muya ni shinai de kudasai yo.

This is a very important matter so please do not try to gloss over it.

雲散霧消 *unsan-mushō*

the clouds scatter, the fog disappears

to go up in a puff of smoke, to disappear without trace, to be scattered on the winds

---

• 例外ばかり認めていたのでは、原則など雲散霧消してしまう。

Reigai bakari mitomete ita no de wa, gensoku nado unsan-mushō shite shimau.

If we allowed all kinds of exceptions to the rule, the general principle would disappear in a puff of smoke.

• バブル経済の崩壊とともに、社屋の移転、新築の話は雲散 霧消した。

Baburu-keizai no hōkai to tomo ni, shaoku no iten, shinchiku no hanashi wa unsan-mushō shita.

When the bubble economy burst, all the talk of companies moving to new premises and erecting new buildings went up in smoke.

栄枯盛衰 *eiko-seisui*

flourish and wither, prosper and perish

the rise and fall of human affairs; the ups and downs of life; the many vicissitudes of life

---

• 栄枯盛衰は世の習いと思ってあきらめるほかないぞ。

Eiko-seisui wa yo no narai to omotte akirameru hoka nai zo.

Son, you have to take the fortunes and misfortunes of life as the way of the world and learn to live with them.

• 「平家物語」は平家の栄枯盛衰を描いている。

"Heike monogatari" wa Heike no eiko-seisui o egaite iru.

The *Heike Monogatari* is a story depicting the rise and fall of the Heike clan.

温故知新 *onko-chishin*

visit the past to know the new (in old Japanese 温 means "to visit")

a study of the classics is the springboard for new research

• 情報の氾濫する現代だからこそ、温故知新の精神を忘れてはいけないと思うよ。

Jōhō no hanran suru gendai da kara koso, onko-chishin no seishin o wasurete wa ikenai to omou yo.

It is precisely because we find ourselves living in an age deluged with information that we must not forget the importance of a thorough grounding in the classics.

- 温故知新のために、世界中の古典を読破したい。

Onko-chishin no tame ni, sekai-jū no koten o dokuha shitai.

To help me pursue my research, I first want to read the classics of world literature to get acquainted with what's gone before.

音信不通 *onshin-futsū*

correspondence interrupted

to lose touch with someone, to be no longer in contact with someone

---

- 何年かは年賀状をやりとりしていたが、今は音信不通だ。

Nannen ka wa nenga-jō o yaritori shite ita ga, ima wa onshin-futsū da.

For many years we sent each other New Year's cards, but now we've lost touch.

- 長い間音信不通になっていた嵯峨さんの消息が分かったよ。

Nagai aida onshin-futsū ni natte ita Saga-san no shōsoku ga wakatta yo.

I got news of ol' Saga the other day; I hadn't heard from him in donkey's years.

外交手腕 *gaikō-shuwan*

diplomatic talent (skill)

diplomacy

- 彼は若いけど見事に外交手腕を発揮して、条約をまとめ上げた。

Kare wa wakai kedo migoto ni gaikō-shuwan o hakki shite, jōyaku o matomeageta.

Though still young, he showed great diplomacy in concluding (drawing up) the treaty.

• 彼の外交手腕には、まったく舌を巻いたよ。

Kare no gaikō-shuwan ni wa, mattaku shita o maita yo.

I have to take my hat off to his tact and diplomacy.

外交辞令 *gaikō-jirei*
diplomatic language
just being polite (diplomatic)

• そんな外交辞令をまともにうける奴があるか。

Sonna gaikō-jirei o matomo ni ukeru yatsu ga aru ka.

Anyone with half a brain could see he was just being diplomatic (polite).

• 単なる外交辞令のつもりだったのに、先方は脈があると思ったらしいんです。

Tannaru gaikō-jirei no tsumori datta no ni, senpō wa myaku ga aru to omotta rashii n' desu.

It was only meant as a polite formality, but it seems the other guy took it as meaning he has a chance.

外柔内剛 *gaijū-naigō*
soft on the outside, hard on the inside
gentle on the outside, tough on the inside; gentle in appearance, but sturdy in spirit (often used to describe people who are hard on themselves but easy on others)

• おとなしそうに見えるのに、頑固なんだよね。典型的な外柔内剛だよ。

Otonashisō ni mieru no ni, ganko nan da yo ne. Tenkei-teki na gaijū-naigō da yo.

She looks like the quiet type, but she's stubborn as hell. She's one of those people who has an easygoing manner but is actually as tough as nails.

● 先生は外柔内剛で、人には優しいが自分には厳しい。

Sensei wa gaijū-naigō de, hito ni wa yasashii ga jibun ni wa kibishii.

Our teacher's kind to others, but he really comes down hard on himself.

→ The opposite to this four-character compound is 内柔外剛 *naijū-gaigō*, which is only different from the above entry in that the first and third characters have changed places.

学歴社会 *gakureki-shakai*

school-record society
a society which places great importance on scholastic credentials and educational background (i.e., which school you went to)

● 学歴社会の弊害が言われて久しいが、一向に改善されていない。

Gakureki-shakai no heigai ga iwarete hisashii ga, ikkō ni kaizen sarete inai.

It's long been said that our society's obsession with academic credentials is harmful, but nothing's ever been done to improve the situation.

● 息子は学歴社会に反発して、大学へは進学しないと言い出した。

Musuko wa gakureki-shakai ni hanpatsu shite, daigaku e wa shingaku shinai to iidashita.

Reacting against the Japanese obsession with scholastic background, our son says he's not going to university.

臥薪嘗胆 *gashin-shōtan*

lying on firewood, licking liver

sustained determination and perseverance; struggling against difficulties for the sake of vengeance; going through thick and thin (fire and water) to avenge oneself against one's enemies

---

• 前回の選挙では落選したが、3年間の臥薪嘗胆の末に当選することができた。

Zenkai no senkyo de wa rakusen shita ga, sannen-kan no gashin-shōtan no sue ni tōsen suru koto ga dekita.

I was a loser in the last election, but I managed to get elected this time after three years of keeping my nose to the grindstone.

• 臥薪嘗胆の浪人生活の末、志望校に合格した。

Gashin-shōtan no rōnin seikatsu no sue, shibō-kō ni gōkaku shita.

Taking a year out to resit my entrance exams was tough, but it paid off in the end when I got accepted by the university I wanted to go to.

→ 浪人 (*rōnin*): In feudal Japan a samurai without a lord and master was called a 浪人 ("a wave-person," being someone condemned to wander about by himself, belonging to no group, a virtual outcast from society). Nowadays this term is used to describe students who are unsuccessful in entering university at the first attempt. Those rōnin who fail their exams two (or three) years running are called 二浪 (*nirō*) or 三浪 (*sanrō*).

❑ In ancient China the Go and the Etsu were at war. After fifteen years of conflict, Kōsen, the Etsu king, led his troops to victory over the Go, whose leader Kōryo was slain in battle. Kōryo's son, Fusa, was determined to avenge his father. Every night he slept on a pile of firewood, to inflame his desire for revenge. It obviously did the trick as within three years he won the Battle of Kaikei, where he defeated the Etsu king Kōsen. Kōsen pleaded for mercy and was allowed to return home after a period of imprisonment. His shame at having surrendered to his fallen foe's son weighed heavily upon him and he resolved to restore his pride the only way he knew how—by beating Fusa in battle. To give himself courage to carry out this endeavor, he covered the floor of his bedroom with the livers of wild animals (in Japanese the character for liver also means courage). He licked up all the liver to give him courage, and thus fortified, set out with his faithful retainer Hanrei to wreak terrible revenge upon Fusa. It took them twenty-two years, but eventually they did it.

我田引水 *gaden-insui*

(to) my ricefield (I) draw water

self-seeking, promoting one's own interests, turning every argument in one's own favor, every miller draws water to his own mill

---

- あいつと話してるといつも我田引水で腹が立つよ。

Aitsu to hanashite 'ru to itsumo gaden-insui de hara ga tatsu yo.

Talking with him drives me up the wall; he's only concerned with looking after his own interests.

- まったく我田引水もいいところだ。

Mattaku gaden-insui mo ii tokoro da.

I've had more than enough of his enlightened self-interest.

- いつも自分に都合のいいようにしかとらないんだな。我田引水もいい加減にしろよ。

Itsumo jibun ni tsugō no ii yō ni shika toranai n' da na. Gaden-insui mo ii kagen ni shiro yo.

You only see things in the best possible light for yourself. Stop being so self-centered.

感情移入 *kanjō-inyū*
emotion moves in
empathy

● 想像力の豊かな人は、感情移入が容易に出来る。

Sōzō-ryoku no yutaka na hito wa, kanjō-inyū ga yōi ni dekiru.

People with vivid imaginations find it easy to empathize with others.

● 相手に感情移入し過ぎては、冷静な判断ができなくなるよ。

Aite ni kanjō-inyū shisugite wa, reisei na handan ga dekinaku naru yo.

If you sympathize with people too much, you won't be able to make rational decisions.

完全無欠 *kanzen-muketsu*
perfect, flawless
absolute perfection, absolutely perfect, faultless, flawless

● お前は完全無欠の女性を求めているから、結婚のチャンスがないんだよ。

Omae wa kanzen-muketsu no josei o motomete iru kara, kekkon no chansu ga nai n' da yo.

You don't have a hope in hell of getting married. You're too busy looking for the perfect woman.

● 今人気があるのは、昔のような完全無欠のヒーローより、むしろどこか抜けている人間的な人だ。

Ima ninki ga aru no wa, mukashi no yō na kanzen-muketsu no hīrō yori, mushiro doko ka nukete iru ningen-teki na hito da.

These days the big crowd-pullers are the slightly wacky kind of guys who are light-years away from the too-good-to-be-true superheroes of old.

➜ You can only use this expression when referring to people. If you want to say a plan is perfect, for example, you have to use a different expression, such as 完璧 (*kanpeki*).

危機一髪 *kiki-ippatsu*

danger (crisis), a hair's breadth (away)

at the critical moment, in the nick of time, a close shave, a close call, by the skin of one's teeth, touch-and-go; to hang by a hair

---

• ホームから線路に落ちた酔っぱらいは、危機一髪のところで救出された。

Hōmu kara senro ni ochita yopparai wa, kiki-ippatsu no toko-ro de kyūshutsu sareta.

The drunkard who toppled off the platform onto the tracks was saved just in the nick of time.

• 危機一髪だったよ。もう少しで浮気がばれるとこだった。

Kiki-ippatsu datta yo. Mō sukoshi de uwaki ga bareru toko datta.

It was a close call, I can tell you. My wife was this far away from finding out about my affair.

• あわや正面衝突かと思ったが、危機一髪で難を免れた。

Awaya shōmen-shōtotsu ka to omotta ga, kiki-ippatsu de nan o manugareta.

I was convinced I was gonna crash right into him but managed to swerve away at the last moment.

➜ This expression is written with the character for hair (髪), but sometimes you might come across it written as 危機一発. This was the punning title given to a 007 James Bond film, with 髪 being replaced by 発 (here meaning a shot from a gun). Due to the film's popularity many people now write the expression this way.

稀少価値 *kishō-kachi*
rareness value
scarcity value

● 今時あんな純情な人、稀少価値があるわね。

Imadoki anna junjō na hito, kishō-kachi ga aru wa ne.

In this day and age people as pure as that are worth their weight in gold.

● そんなにきれいじゃないけど、稀少価値があるから高価なんだ。

Sonna ni kirei ja nai kedo, kishō-kachi ga aru kara kōka nan da.

It's not that beautiful to look at, but it is valuable because of its rarity.

➜ This expression can also be written as 希少価値.

喜色満面 *kishoku-manmen*
a joyful color fills (one's) face
a face full of joy, beaming with joy, all smiles and joy, smiling from ear to ear, delight written all over one's face, a face lit up with joy, grinning like a Cheshire cat, as pleased as Punch

---

● 祐二はたくさんお年玉をもらって、喜色満面だった。

Yūji wa takusan otoshidama o moratte, kishoku-manmen datta.

With all the money he'd received from his relatives over the New Year, Yuji looked as pleased as Punch.

❏ お年玉 (*otoshidama*) is the traditional gift of money given by parents (and other adult relations) to their children at New Year.

• 父は露天風呂に入りながら喜色満面で熱燗を飲んでいる。

Chichi wa rotenburo ni hairinagara, kishoku-manmen de atsukan o nonde iru.

Dad's sitting out in the open-air bath drinking hot sake with a look of profound contentment on his face.

❏ 露天風呂 (*rotenburo*) is an open-air bath at a hot spring, of which there are many all over Japan. It is sometimes jokingly said that a Japanese man is happiest when sipping hot sake (*atsukan*) in a hot *rotenburo* (at which point he is supposed to say 極楽、極楽 [*gokuraku, gokuraku*], which means "Ah, what paradise!").

• 連戦連勝で、監督は喜色満面だね。

Rensen-renshō de, kantoku wa kishoku-manmen da ne.

Our manager's all smiles because of our recent unbeaten streak.

得意満面 *tokui-manmen*
a face full of pride
looking pleased with yourself, looking smug, strutting about like a peacock, be as proud as a peacock

---

• 息子は第 1 志望校に合格して、得意満面だよ。

Musuko wa daiichi-shibōkō ni gōkaku shite, tokui-manmen da yo.

When our son got into his first-choice university, he went round looking as proud as a peacock.

• あいつ、ちょっとほめられたと思って、得意満面になってるぜ。

Aitsu, chotto homerareta to omotte, tokui-manmen ni natte 'ru ze.

He thinks he's the cat's whiskers just because he got a pat on the back.

→ 喜色満面 is a neutral expression used to describe someone who looks happy. However 得意満面 is used pejoratively to imply that the person is a bit too pleased. It is often used when criticizing or simply teasing someone.

疑心暗鬼 *gishin-anki*

a suspicious mind (produces) dark demons

a feeling of suspicion (a doubt) gnaws at one, suspicions eat away at one, paranoid

---

• イアゴーの告げ口が、オセロの胸に疑心暗鬼を生じさせた。

Iagō no tsugeguchi ga, Osero no mune ni gishin-anki o shōji-saseta.

Iago's talebearing awakened in Othello's heart a terrible suspicion.

• 親友が僕の悪口を陰で言いふらしていると聞いて、疑心暗鬼に陥ったよ。

Shin'yū ga boku no warukuchi o kage de iifurashite iru to kiite, gishin-anki ni ochiitta yo.

When I heard that a good friend was bad-mouthing me behind my back, I felt that I could no longer trust anyone.

• 連絡が遅いから、何かあったんじゃないかと、疑心暗鬼になっていたんだ。

Renraku ga osoi kara, nani ka atta n' ja nai ka to, gishin-anki ni natte ita n' da.

As time ticked on and still no word came, I began to think something awful must have happened.

奇想天外 *kisō-tengai*

an unusual idea (falls down from) the sky
fantastic, out of the ordinary

• あんな奇想天外な作戦が、まさか成功するとは思わなかったよ。

Anna kisō-tengai na sakusen ga, masaka seikō suru to wa omo-wanakatta yo.

I would never have believed that such a weird strategy would work out so well.

• ずいぶんと奇想天外なデザインだけど、買う人いるのかなあ。

Zuibun to kisō-tengai na dezain da kedo, kau hito iru no ka nā.

It's a pretty off-the-wall design, but are people gonna want to buy it?

喜怒哀楽 *kido-airaku*

joy, anger, sadness, and pleasure
(the gamut of) human emotions

• 彼があんなに喜怒哀楽を見せるとは、意外だったなあ。

Kare ga anna ni kido-airaku o miseru to wa, igai datta nā.

It was a real surprise to see him show such emotion.

• 普段は一切喜怒哀楽を表情に出さない人なのにね。

Fudan wa issai kido-airaku o hyōjō ni dasanai hito na no ni ne.

Usually he never shows the slightest trace of emotion.

• 昔は、喜怒哀楽の情を露にするのは、はしたないと教えられたものだよ。

Mukashi wa, kido-airaku no jō o arawa ni suru no wa, hashitanai to oshierareta mono da yo.

In the old days we were always taught that showing your feelings (giving vent to your emotions) was just not done.

旧態依然 *kyūtai-izen*

(in the same) old style as ever

the old school, things remain just as they have always been, a stick-in-the-mud, reactionary, fuddy-duddy, old-fashioned

---

• 若いのに、どうしてそんな旧態依然とした考え方しかできないの？

Wakai no ni, dōshite sonna kyūtai-izen to shita kangaekata shika dekinai no?

For somebody so young, how come you've got such a stick-in-the-mud attitude?

• 経営陣の頭が旧態依然のコチコチだから、もううちの社も長くないよ。

Keiei-jin no atama ga kyūtai-izen no kochikochi da kara, mō uchi no sha mo nagaku nai yo.

Our company's gonna go under soon; the guys at the top have got a mind-set so out-of-date it's almost Neanderthal.

共存共栄 *kyōzon-kyōei*

living together, flourishing together

co-existence and co-prosperity

• 下請けを利用するというのではなく、共存共栄して行くという考え方でなければだめさ。

Shitauke o riyō suru to iu no de wa naku, kyōzon-kyōei shite iku to iu kangaekata de nakereba dame sa.

We're not out to exploit our sub-contractors; if we don't work together with them, none of us is gonna do well.

• 自国さえ繁栄すればよいのではなく、他の国々と共存共栄
していきたい。

*Jikoku sae han'ei sureba yoi no de wa naku, ta no kuniguni to
kyōson-kyōei shite ikitai.*

Just for our own country to be prosperous is not enough; we
want to live and work together in harmony with all countries.

器用貧乏 *kiyō-binbō*
dexterous and poor
Jack of all trades and master of none, fixer-upper,
handyman, talented amateur

• 彼は何でも一応要領よくこなすんだけど、しょせん器用貧
乏なんだよね。

*Kare wa nan de mo ichiō yōryō yoku konasu n' da kedo, sho-
sen kiyō-binbō nan da yo ne.*

He can take on anything and do a decent job, but when all is
said and done he's nothing but a fixer-upper.

• 器用貧乏って言われたくないから、何か一つのことを徹底
的にマスターしたいんだ。

*Kiyō-binbō tte iwaretaku nai kara, nanika hitotsu no koto o
tettei-teki ni masutā shitai n' da.*

I don't want to be thought of as "a Jack of all trades but master
of none," so I'm going to make myself into an expert at
something.

玉石混淆 *gyokuseki-konkō*
jewels and stones mixed together
a mixture of the good and the bad

● 新入社員も、以前は粒が揃っていたけど、このごろじゃ玉
石混淆だよ。

Shinnyū-shain mo, izen wa tsubu ga sorotte ita kedo, kono goro ja gyokuseki-konkō da yo.

We always used to get a well-balanced crop of new recruits in the old days, but of late it's been a mixed bag.

● どんな有名作家の作品でも、やはりある程度は玉石混淆に
なりますね。

Donna yūmei-sakka no sakuhin de mo, yahari aru teido wa gyokuseki-konkō ni narimasu ne.

It doesn't matter how famous the writer is, there will always be some second-rate work mixed in with the masterpieces.

➜ This expression can also be written as 玉石混交.

拒絶反応 *kyozetsu-hannō*
refusal reaction
rejection (of foreign tissue or organ); adverse reaction

● 移植手術は成功したが、拒絶反応が心配だ。

Ishoku-shujutsu wa seikō shita ga, kyozetsu-hannō ga shinpai da.

The transplant operation was a success, but we're still worried about possible rejection.

● 拒絶反応さえ抑えられれば、回復するんだが。

Kyozetsu-hannō sae osaerareba, kaifuku suru n' da ga.

As long as we can keep the rejection symptoms under control, there's a good chance of recovery.

● 外国語と聞くと、拒絶反応を起こしてしまうようだよ。

Gaikoku-go to kiku to, kyozetsu-hannō o okoshite shimau yō da yo.

The words "foreign language" are enough to bring him out in a cold sweat.

- 原子力の利用には拒絶反応を起こす人が多い。

Genshi-ryoku no riyō ni wa kyozetsu-hannō o okosu hito ga ōi.

There are a lot of people who feel violently opposed to the use of nuclear power.

→ A synonymous expression (when used in the figurative sense given in the last two examples) is 拒否反応 (*kyohi-hannō*).

毀誉褒貶 *kiyo-hōhen*

praise and criticism

mixed opinion, divergent views, one extreme or the other

- この政治家は、見方によって毀誉褒貶いろいろだ。

Kono seiji-ka wa, mikata ni yotte kiyo-hōhen iroiro da.

Depending on your point of view, that politician's either a hero or a crook.

- 毀誉褒貶は世の習いと言うけれど、それにしてもこの人の評判は両極端だね。

Kiyo-hōhen wa yo no narai to iu keredo, sore ni shite mo kono hito no hyōban wa ryō-kyokutan da ne.

They say you can't please all the people all of the time, but even so, opinions on this guy run to extremes.

金権政治 *kinken-seiji*

power-of-money politics

money politics; plutocracy

- 選挙の度に金権政治の打破が叫ばれるが、結局何も変わっちゃいない。

Senkyo no tabi ni kinken-seiji no daha ga sakebareru ga, kekkyoku nani mo kawatcha inai.

Every time there's an election there's lots of talk about doing away with money politics, but in the end nothing ever changes.

- このところ投票率が下がり続けているのは、国民が金権政治に愛想をつかしたからだろう。

Kono tokoro tōhyō-ritsu ga sagaritsuzukete iru no wa, kokumin ga kinken-seiji ni aiso o tsukashita kara darō.

The reason why the voter turnout keeps going down, I suppose, is because the general public is fed up with money politics.

苦心惨憺 *kushin-santan*

take pains, trouble one's heart

much hard work and effort; 〜する to take great pains, to go to a lot of trouble (to get something done), to struggle hard

---

- 苦心惨憺の結果、ようやくライフワークの『日本語方言大辞典』が完成した。

Kushin-santan no kekka, yōyaku raifuwāku no "Nihongo Hōgen Dai-jiten" ga kansei shita.

After much toil and effort she at last completed her lifework, *A Dictionary of Japanese Dialects.*

- 倉橋教授は何度も失敗して苦心惨憺したが、ついに新薬開発に成功した。

Kurahashi-kyōju wa nando mo shippai shite kushin-santan shita ga, tsui ni shin'yaku-kaihatsu ni seikō shita.

After a long hard struggle and many failures, Professor Kurahashi at last succeeded in developing the new drug.

• まったく苦心惨憺させられたぜ、あいつには。

Mattaku kushin-santan saserareta ze, aitsu ni wa.

I was really put through the wringer on account of that jerk.

➜ Synonymous expressions include 悪戦苦闘 (*akusen-kutō*) and 四苦八苦 (*shiku-hakku*).

厚顔無恥 *kōgan-muchi*
a thick face and no shame
impudent, shameless, brazen, cheeky, unscrupulous, barefaced

• あんな厚顔無恥な奴とは思ってもみなかった。俺も人を見る目がないよ。

Anna kōgan-muchi na yatsu to wa omotte mo minakatta. Ore mo hito o miru me ga nai yo.

I would never have thought he was such an unscrupulous bastard. I'm obviously no great judge of character.

• なんて図々しい！　厚顔無恥って、あの人のためにある言葉じゃないかしら。

Nante zūzūshii! Kōgan-muchi tte, ano hito no tame ni aru kotoba ja nai kashira.

What nerve! He's the sort of guy that the expression "barefaced cheek" was invented for.

荒唐無稽 *kōtō-mukei*
pointless and groundless
absurd, nonsensical, wild

• そんな荒唐無稽な話を誰が信じるもんか。

Sonna kōtō-mukei na hanashi o dare ga shinjiru mon ka.

Who's ever going to believe a story as crazy as that?

● かれらは本気であの荒唐無稽な説明を繰り返しているんだ。

Karera wa honki de ano kōtō-mukei na setsumei o kurikaeshite iru n' da.

They're sticking to that cock and bull story as if they really believed it,

● SFは、合理的であるより荒唐無稽なくらいの方が面白いよ。

Esuefu wa, gōri-teki de aru yori kōtō-mukei na kurai no hō ga omoshiroi yo.

Science fiction that verges on the absurd is much more interesting than the rational (realistic) stuff.

呉越同舟 *goetsu-dōshū*
The Go and the Etsu in the same boat
bitter enemies (placed by fate) in the same boat, adversity makes strange bedfellows, to be united by ties of common interest

---

● 元の与党と野党第1党が、呉越同舟の連立内閣を組んだ。

Moto no yotō to yatō daiittō ga, goetsu-dōshū no renritsu-naikaku o kunda.

The cabinet was formed by a coalition of convenience between the former ruling party and their ex-arch rivals, who used to be the main opposition party.

● あの二人が一緒にゴルフに行ったとは、呉越同舟だね。

Ano futari ga issho ni gorufu ni itta to wa, goetsu-dōshū da ne.

Those two hate each other's guts, so it's odd they should go off and play golf together.

❑ The Go and the Etsu were two rival states in ancient China which were always at war with each other.

極楽往生 *gokuraku-ōjō*

rebirth in paradise

an extremely pleasant death, a painless death, to leave
(this world) and be reborn in paradise, to die peace-
fully (in one's bed), to pass away in peace

• 極楽往生を願っていたおじいさんは、苦しまずに亡くなった。

*Gokuraku-ōjō o negatte ita ojīsan wa, kurushimazu ni naku-
natta.*

Grandpa had always hoped for a peaceful death and that's
what he got, slipping away quietly and painlessly.

❑ Originally used to mean being reborn in Buddhist heaven
after leaving this world. Now used to mean simply to die a
peaceful death. In addition, someone who is a care-free,
happy-go-lucky type is mockingly called *gokuraku-tonbo* 極楽
とんぼ (a paradise dragonfly).

五里霧中 *gori-muchū*

five ri *in the fog*

in a fog, all at sea, bewildered, at a total loss (what to
do); to not have the foggiest idea what to do, to not
have a clue

• 初めてフランスへ行った時は、全然言葉が分からなくて、
五里霧中でしたよ。

*Hajimete Furansu e itta toki wa, zenzen kotoba ga wakara-
nakute, gori-muchū deshita yo.*

The first time I went to France, I couldn't understand a word
of what was being said. I was totally at sea.

• 畑違いの企画を任されて、いまだに五里霧中の状態なんです。

Hatake-chigai no kikaku o makasarete, imada ni gori-muchū no jōtai nan desu.

They've put me in charge of a project that's outside my field. I still haven't got a clue what I should be doing.

❑ A *ri* is a unit of distance (approximately equivalent to two and a half miles) that was used in ancient China and Japan. This four-character compound is said to derive from the trick once practised by a Chinese mystic of conjuring up a thick fog to engulf his enemies and make them lose their sense of direction. Care should taken when writing this expression as people sometimes confuse the third character with the character for dream (夢), whose *on*-reading is also *mu*. Perhaps this is because in Japanese the compound 夢中 (*muchū*) is commonly used in the phrase 夢中になる, which means to become engrossed/absorbed in (something).

言語道断 *gongo-dōdan*

words cannot express (originally "the ultimate truth of Buddha's teaching cannot be expressed by (mere) words," but now used pejoratively)

unspeakable, unutterable, unmentionable, outrageous, unpardonable, inexcusable, preposterous, absurd, abominable, shocking, scandalous, beyond description

---

• こんな初歩的なミスだらけのレポートを出すなんて、言語道断だね。

Konna shoho-teki na misu darake no repōto o dasu nante, gongo-dōdan da ne.

It is inexcusable to hand in a report so full of rudimentary mistakes as this.

• 「金さえ払えば文句なかろう」だと？言語道断な言い種だ。

"Kane sae haraeba monku nakarō" da to? Gongo-dōdan na iigusa da.

What do you mean "I'm paying, so what do you have to complain about?" What a despicable thing to say!

才色兼備 *saishoku-kenbi*

equipped with both brains and beauty
blessed (gifted, endowed) with both brains and beauty
(mostly in reference to women)

• 結婚式のスピーチでは、どんな人でも才色兼備になっちゃうんだよね。

Kekkon-shiki no supīchi de wa, donna hito de mo saishoku-kenbi ni natchau n' da yo ne.

In wedding speeches, no matter what the bride is like, she is said to be blessed with both brains and beauty.

• 彼女みたいに才色兼備でしかも家が金持ちって人見ると、神様は不公平だと思うわ。

Kanojo mitai ni saishoku-kenbi de shikamo uchi ga kanemochi tte hito miru to, kamisama wa fu-kōhei da to omou wa.

When I see people like her who are intelligent, beautiful, and from a wealthy background, I can't help thinking God isn't quite fair.

三角関係 *sankaku-kankei*

a triangular relationship
a love triangle

• 三角関係のもつれから、男が妻の愛人を殺すという事件が起こった。

Sankaku-kankei no motsure kara, otoko ga tsuma no aijin o korosu to iu jiken ga okotta.

There was a case (recently) of a guy killing his wife's lover after they got involved in a love triangle.

- 親友の彼氏と付き合い始めちゃって、今どろどろの三角関係なんだよね。

Shin'yū no kareshi to tsukiaihajimechatte, ima dorodoro sankaku-kankei nan da yo ne.

I started going out with my best friend's boyfriend, and now we're involved in this messy triangular relationship.

- そろそろ三角関係を清算しなくちゃと思うんだが、二人ともいいところがあって捨て難いんだ。

Sorosoro sankaku-kankei o seisan shinakucha to omou n' da ga, futari tomo ii tokoro ga atte sutegatai n' da.

Pretty soon I'm gonna have to put a end to this triangular relationship. The thing is, they both have good points and I hate to chuck either one of them.

三寒四温 *sankan-shion*

three cold days (followed by) four warm days
a cycle of three cold days and four warm days

- 立春も過ぎ、三寒四温のすごしやすい季節となりましたが、お元気ですか。

Risshun mo sugi, sankan-shion no sugoshiyasui kisetsu to narimashita ga, ogenki desu ka.

The vernal equinox has come and gone. Winter's chill is slowly giving way to the warmth of spring, as we enter this most pleasant time of the year. How are you keeping? (This is a traditional greeting in letters written toward the end of February.)

- 三寒四温のこのころが、一年中で一番好きだよ。

Sankan-shion no kono koro ga, ichinen-jū de ichiban suki da yo.

This is my favorite time of year, as the cold days of winter gradually recede to be replaced by the warmth of spring.

三拝九拝 *sanpai-kyūhai*

three bows, nine bows

to bow many times, to kowtow, (to ask a favor) on bended knee, to bow and scrape, to fall on one's knees

- 彼女のおやじさんに三拝九拝して、やっと結婚を許してもらった。

Kanojo no oyaji-san ni sanpai-kyūhai shite, yatto kekkon o yurushite moratta.

After I begged on bended knee, my girlfriend's father finally consented to our marriage.

- 三拝九拝して、せっかくもらってきた注文なのに、在庫がないなんてついてないよ。

Sanpai-kyūhai shite, sekkaku moratte kita chūmon na no ni, zaiko ga nai nante tsuite 'nai yo.

After a lot of bowing and scraping I finally get the order and what happens? We're out of stock. It's just not my day.

自画自賛 *jiga-jisan*

(one's) own drawing, (one's) own praise

～する to blow one's own trumpet, to sing one's own praises; to pat oneself on the back

- この人の回想録は自画自賛の話ばかりで、おもしろくも何ともない。

Kono hito no kaisō-roku wa jiga-jisan no hanashi bakari de, omoshiroku mo nan to mo nai.

His memoirs are as dull as ditch water; all he does is paint a pretty picture of himself.

おばあちゃんは近ごろ俳句に凝っていて、一句出来る度に自画自賛してるよ。

Obāchan wa chikagoro haiku ni kotte ite, ikku dekiru tabi ni jiga-jisan shite 'ru yo.

Granny's become really keen on haiku recently. It's funny—every time she writes a new one, she pats herself on the back.

❏ This expression derives from the practice of one's teacher writing a few words of praise in the corner of one's painting, and then adding his seal (of approval) to authenticate the comments as his own. Without this favorable comment from one's sensei, a picture has little value. To add the all-important critique oneself is not only highly disreputable but also self-serving and smug.

時期尚早 *jiki-shōsō*
the timing is too early
the time is not yet ripe for (doing something), to jump the gun, to be premature

---

• 今からそんな心配までするのは、時期尚早というものだよ。

Ima kara sonna shinpai made suru no wa, jiki-shōsō to iu mono da yo.

It's much too early to be getting all worried about that now.

• 時代を先取りした法律だったが、時期尚早だという声が多く、廃案になってしまった。

Jidai o sakidori shita hōritsu datta ga, jiki-shōsō da to iu koe ga ōku, haian ni natte shimatta.

The law was made with an eye to the future, but it was repealed when many voiced the opinion that it was ahead of its time.

自給自足 *jikyū-jisoku*
self-providing, self-satisfying
self-sufficiency, self-supporting, self-reliant; 〜する to
be self-sufficient

• 自給自足の生活って、実際にはそりゃ大変らしいよ。

Jikyū-jisoku no seikatsu tte, jissai ni wa sorya taihen rashii yo.

Seems trying to live a life of self-sufficiency is really tough.

• この国の農業は、まだ自給自足の段階に達していない。

Kono kuni no nōgyō wa, mada jikyū-jisoku no dankai ni tasshite inai.

This country's nowhere near being agriculturally self-sufficient.

• いざという時に、自給自足でやっていける国がいくつあるだろうか。

Iza to iu toki ni, jikyū-jisoku de yatte ikeru kuni ga ikutsu aru darō ka.

If push came to shove, I wonder how many countries could really get by without outside help.

• 友だちに、会社を辞めて田舎に古い家買って、自給自足してる奴がいるよ。

Tomodachi ni, kaisha o yamete inaka ni furui ie katte, jikyū-jisoku shite 'ru yatsu ga iru yo.

I've got this friend who quit his job, bought an old house out in the country, and is now living off the land.

• 食料の自給自足体制が整っていないわが国では、食料安保が大きな問題だ。

Shokuryō no jikyū-jisoku taisei ga totonotte inai wagakuni de wa, shokuryō-anpo ga ōkina mondai da.

Since the country has no system of self-sufficiency to fall back on, we have to consider the need for a treaty guaranteeing sufficient food supplies.

❑ Agricultural self-sufficiency is a Japanese worry that Westerners often find difficult to understand. Many Japanese (especially those who lived through the Second World War when food was in short supply) still feel it is essential that Japan be able to produce enough food (in particular, rice) to feed itself, without relying upon imports. This perhaps accounts in part for the fact that they are prepared to buy home-grown rice rather than imported rice, even though it is more than twice the price.

四苦八苦 *shiku-hakku*

four pains, eight pains

to writhe in agony, to be in dire distress, to sweat blood

• 好きな作家の新作が出たんだけど、まだ翻訳がないから、読み終えるのに四苦八苦したよ。

Suki na sakka no shinsaku ga deta n' da kedo, mada hon'yaku ga nai kara, yomioeru no ni shiku-hakku shita yo.

One of my favorite authors came out with a new book, but since there's no translation yet, I had to sweat blood to get through it.

• 中年サラリーマンの多くが、マイホームのローンと子供の教育費に四苦八苦している。

Chūnen-sararīman no ōku ga, maihōmu no rōn to kodomo no kyōiku-hi ni shiku-hakku shite iru.

A lot of middle-aged white-collar workers have a devil of a time paying for the mortgage and the kids' education.

→ This expression is synonymous with 悪戦苦闘 (*akusen-kutō*).

❑ In Buddhism the four types of pain that are considered to be the root causes of human suffering are (1) the pain of birth, (2) the pain of sickness and ill health, (3) the pain of old age, (4) the pain of death. In addition, there are four further types of pain, which are (1) 愛別離苦 (*aibetsu-riku*) the pain of being away from the ones you love, (2) 怨憎会苦 (*onzō-eku*) the pain of meeting with things you dislike, (3) 求不得苦 (*gufu-tokuku*) the pain of not getting what you want, (4) 五陰盛苦 (*goon-jōku*) mental and physical pain. These eight types of pain are the 八苦 referred to in this four-character compound.

試行錯誤 *shikō-sakugo*
trial undertaking, confused failure
trial and error

- 前例もないし、今はまだ試行錯誤の段階ですよ。

Zenrei mo nai shi, ima wa mada shikō-sakugo no dankai desu yo.

There's no precedent to help us, so for the moment we're still at the trial-and-error stage.

- 試行錯誤を繰り返して、やっと自分にあったやり方がわかってきたような気がします。

Shikō-sakugo o kurikaeshite, yatto jibun ni atta yarikata ga wakatte kita yō na ki ga shimasu.

After repeated trial and error, I finally feel that I've found the method that suits me best.

自業自得 *jigō-jitoku*
self-deed, self-gain (one's own deeds, one's own rewards)
you reap what you sow; you made your bed, now you have to lie in it; you've got nobody to blame but yourself; you deserve what you get; it serves you right; you asked for it

---

- こう言っちゃ何だが、あいつが破産したのは自業自得さ。

Kō itcha nan da ga, aitsu ga hasan shita no wa jigō-jitoku sa.

I suppose I shouldn't say this, but if he's gone bankrupt, he's only got himself to blame.

- 勉強せずにファミコンばかりしてたんだから、試験に落ちても自業自得だよ。

Benkyō sezu ni famikon bakari shite 'ta n' da kara, shiken ni ochite mo jigō-jitoku da yo.

Since you were playing computer games all the time instead of studying, it'll be your own fault if you fail the exams.

自己陶酔 *jiko-tōsui*
self-intoxication
self-conceit, self-admiration, to think yourself the center of the universe, to be in love with yourself, to be narcissistic

---

- 自己陶酔してるんじゃないの。馬鹿みたい。

Jiko-tōsui shite 'ru n' ja nai no. Baka mitai.

I'd stop thinking I was God Almighty if I were you. Grow up!

- あの時代は甘っちょろい自己陶酔にひたっている暇はなかった。

Ano jidai wa amatchoroi jiko-tōsui ni hitatte iru hima wa nakatta.

In that day and age there just wasn't time for us to get carried away with our own brilliance (with any inflated sense of our own worth).

自己満足 *jiko-manzoku*
self-satisfaction
complacent satisfaction with oneself or one's accomplishments, self-congratulation, smugness

---

• おだてられて、自己満足してるだけだよ。

Odaterarete, jiko-manzoku shite 'ru dake da yo.

A little flattery, and look how proud he is of himself.

• 単なる自己満足に終わってしまっては、進歩がないな。

Tannaru jiko-manzoku ni owatte shimatte wa, shinpo ga nai na.

If it ends up as an exercise in self-satisfaction, nothing will be achieved at all.

四捨五入 *shisha-gonyū*
throw away the fours, put in the fives
to round to the nearest whole number, dropping anything below five

---

• 若いつもりでいてももう25、四捨五入したら30だもんね。

Wakai tsumori de ite mo mō nijū-go, shisha-gonyū shitara sanjū da mon ne.

At 25 I like to think of myself as still being young, but rounded off it comes to 30.

• 100円以下は切り捨てますか、切り上げますか、それとも四捨五入しますか。

Hyaku-en ika wa kirisutemasu ka, kiriagemasu ka, sore tomo shisha-gonyū shimasu ka.

Are we going to round down amounts of less than 100 yen, or round them up? Or are we going to round up anything over 50 and round down the rest?

自信満々 *jishin-manman*
full of confidence
brimming with confidence, supremely confident

● 試験の前は自信満々だったが、手も足も出なくて惨めだった。

Shiken no mae wa jishin-manman datta ga, te mo ashi mo denakute mijime datta.

Before the exam I was brimming with confidence, but I just wasn't up to it and failed miserably.

● 彼女、スタイルには自信満々で、いつも体にぴったりの服着てる。

Kanojo, sutairu ni wa jishin-manman de, itsumo karada ni pittari no fuku kite 'ru.

She's supremely confident of her good figure and always wears tight-fitting clothes.

七転八倒 *shichiten-battō*
falling over seven times, collapsing eight times
writhing in agony, to be in excruciating pain

● 急に胸が痛くなって、病院に運ばれるまで七転八倒の苦しみだった。

Kyū ni mune ga itaku natte, byōin ni hakobareru made shichiten-battō no kurushimi datta.

I felt this sudden pain in my chest and until they got me to the hospital, I was in excruciating agony.

● 畳の上で脂汗を流しながら七転八倒しているところへ、家内が帰って来てくれてね。

Tatami no ue de abura-ase o nagashinagara shichiten-battō shite iru tokoro e, kanai ga kaette kite kurete ne.

Luckily my wife came home when she did; she found me
writhing in agony on the floor, covered in sweat.

患者は鎮痛剤が切れて、七転八倒の苦しみようだった。

*Kanja wa chintsū-zai ga kirete, shichiten-battō no kurushimiyō
datta.*

Once the anesthetic had worn off, the patient was in real
agony.

叱咤激励 *shitta-gekirei*

*scolding, encouraging (encouragement with a berat-
ing voice)*

〜する to give somebody a pep talk, to psyche them
up, to fire them up, to get them going, to put some fire
in their belly

• 監督は声を張り上げて、選手たちを叱咤激励した。

Kantoku wa koe o hariagete, senshu-tachi o shitta-gekirei shita.

The manager screamed his head off, trying to get his team
psyched up.

• 皆様から叱咤激励をいただいて頑張りたいと思います。

*Minasama kara shitta-gekirei o itadaite ganbaritai to omoi-
masu.*

With everyone's encouragement and advice, I will endeavor to
do the very best I can.

• 若い人を叱咤激励して、やる気にさせるのもなかなか大変
だよ。

*Wakai hito o shitta-gekirei shite, yaru ki ni saseru no mo
nakanaka taihen da yo.*

Trying to encourage young people to get up and do something
is no piece of cake.

• 自分で自分を叱咤激励しながら、今日までやって来ました。

Jibun de jibun o shitta-gekirei shinagara, kyō made yatte kimashita.

I got where I am today by spurring myself on all along the way.

十中八九 *jitchū-hakku*
eight or nine out of ten
ten to one; in nine cases out of ten; in all probability

• 十中八九間違いないと思いますが、もう一度確認の電話を入れてみます。

Jitchū-hakku machigai nai to omoimasu ga, mō ichido kakunin no denwa o irete mimasu.

There's next to no mistake about it, but I'll call once more just to be sure.

• 最終面接まで行ったんだったら、もう十中八九内定だよ。

Saishū-mensetsu made itta n' dattara, mō jitchū-hakku naitei da yo.

If they asked you to come in for the final interview, you've almost got the job sewn up, I'm sure.

→ The expression 九分九厘 (*kubu-kurin*) is virtually synonymous. Its degree of certainty is a bit higher (at 99%) than 十中八九 (80–90%), but in general the two expressions are used interchangeably, both meaning "almost definitely."

自暴自棄 *jibō-jiki*
self-abuse, self-abandonment
desperation, despair; 〜になる to abandon oneself to despair, to be in total despair

---

• あいつ彼女にふられて以来、自暴自棄になってるみたいだぜ。

Aitsu kanojo ni furarete irai, jibō-jiki ni natte 'ru mitai da ze.

It seems he's been in total despair ever since he was given the elbow by his girlfriend.

• その程度のことで、そんなに自暴自棄になる必要はないのに……。

Sono teido no koto de, sonna ni jibō-jiki ni naru hitsuyō wa nai no ni ...

I don't know why you have to get all bent out of shape over some little thing like that.

❏ The last two characters of this compound (自棄) can also be pronounced *yake* when written as a two-character compound (though nowadays most people write this simply as やけ, using hiragana). The meaning is the same as above, and it is commonly used in the expressions やけになる (*yake ni naru*; to feel desperate and lose control of oneself) and やけ酒を飲む (*yakezake o nomu*; to drown one's sorrows in drink or take to drink out of desperation).

四方八方 *shihō-happō*
four directions, eight directions
in all directions, in every direction, far and wide, every which way, (from) all quarters, (from) all over

---

• 発表と同時に四方八方から引き合いが来て、嬉しい悲鳴を上げてるんだ。

Happyō to dōji ni shihō-happō kara hikiai ga kite, ureshii himei o agete 'ru n da.

Since the announcement was made, we have been inundated with inquiries and positively overwhelmed by the response.

• 娘が家出して以来、四方八方手を尽くして探してるんだが、全く行方が知れない。

Musume ga iede shite irai, shihō-happō te o tsukushite saga-shite 'ru n' da ga, mattaku yukue ga shirenai.

We've left no stone unturned, but still we have no idea of my daughter's whereabouts since she ran away from home.

❑ The four directions referred to in the first half of this four-character compound—四方—are the four points of the compass. Add northeast, northwest, southeast, and southwest, and you end up with a total of eight different directions—八方.

島国根性 *shimaguni-konjō*

island country mentality

an island-nation mentality, insularism, insularity

• イギリス人と日本人の国民性はずいぶん違うけど、一つ共通してるのは島国根性だね。

Igirisu-jin to nihon-jin no kokumin-sei wa zuibun chigau kedo, hitotsu kyōtsū shite 'ru no wa shimaguni-konjō da ne.

The British and the Japanese have quite different national characteristics, but one thing they do have in common is their insular mentality.

• 経済的に大国になったのに、いつまでたっても島国根性が抜けないでいる。

Keizai-teki ni taikoku ni natta no ni, itsu made tatte mo shima-guni-konjō ga nukenai de iru.

Even though Japan has become an economic superpower, we just can't seem to free ourselves of our insularity.

➡ The opposite to this is 大陸的な (*tairiku-teki na*), which literally means "continental" and refers to peoples who are generous of spirit and who do not fuss about trifles.

四面楚歌 *shimen-soka*

(on) all four sides (can be heard) the So song

surrounded on all sides by one's enemies, without a friend in the world, all alone without a single ally (in sight), under siege, besieged

- 会議の席で上司を非難してしまい、四面楚歌の立場に追込まれてしまった。

Kaigi no seki de jōshi o hinan shite shimai, shimen-soka no tachiba ni oikomarete shimatta.

After criticizing the boss at the meeting I found myself being cold-shouldered by everyone in the office.

- 女房も子供もおふくろも、皆俺のせいだって言うんだ。まったく四面楚歌だよ。

Nyōbō mo kodomo mo ofukuro mo, minna ore no sei datte iu n' da. Mattaku shimen-soka da yo.

The wife and kids and even my own Mom are all convinced it's my fault; no one's taking my side at all.

❑ In ancient China Ryuho (the founder of the Kan dynasty) and his arch-rival Kō, a mighty warrior of great strength and the warlord of the So region, were locked in a bitter power struggle to become emperor. By 202 BC the balance of power was in Ryuho's favor, and Kō found himself facing severe difficulties.

Kō was surrounded in his garrison at Gaika (in An Hui province in present-day China) by Kan troops under the command of Kanshin, one of Ryuho's most able generals. One evening Kanshin thought up a plan to break the will of his still powerful enemy. He got his men to sing a So folk song in a sad and mournful way. When Kō heard this, he immediately assumed that Ryuho had overrun the So region and taken all Kō's followers prisoner, and that it was they who were singing. Convinced that he had lost his power base and the war was as good as over, Kō committed suicide.

自問自答 *jimon-jitō*

ask oneself, answer oneself

a soliloquy, a monologue, thinking aloud; 〜する to think aloud, to wonder to oneself, to ask oneself

---

● どこで間違ったのかと自問自答してみたが、答えは出なかった。

Doko de machigatta no ka to jimon-jitō shite mita ga, kotae wa denakatta.

I wondered to myself where I might have gone wrong, but I just couldn't think of an answer.

● これからどうしたらいいかと、彼は長い間自問自答して、結局は田舎に帰ることにした。

Kore kara dō shitara ii ka to, kare wa nagai aida jimon-jitō shite, kekkyoku wa inaka ni kaeru koto ni shita.

After long deliberation as to what he should do from now on, he finally decided to go back to his hometown.

弱肉強食 *jakuniku-kyōshoku*

the weak (are) meat (for) the strong (to) eat

the law of the jungle, the survival of the fittest, only the strong survive, it's a dog-eat-dog world

---

● 野生動物は、弱肉強食の自然界で生きている。

Yasei-dōbutsu wa, jakuniku-kyōshoku no shizen-kai de ikite iru.

Wild animals inhabit a world where the only law is eat or be eaten. (Animals in the wild live according to the law of the jungle.)

● きれいごとを言ったって、所詮世の中は弱肉強食なんだよ。

Kireigoto o itta tte, shosen yo no naka wa jakuniku-kyōshoku nan da yo.

For all your fine words, it is still a dog-eat-dog world.

❏ In Japanese schools, students are often tested on their knowledge of four-letter compounds. They are sometimes presented with compounds with two of their component characters missing, and have to fill in the blanks correctly. In the case of 弱肉強食 the first and third characters are usually left blank (i.e., □肉□食). In one apocryphal case a hungry fifteen-year-old was said to have written 焼肉定食 (*yakiniku-teishoku*; a popular and inexpensive lunch of Korean-style beef served with rice and miso soup). Obviously his concerns in life were more culinary than classical.

自由自在 *jiyū-jizai*

free and at will

freely, to one's heart's desire, with wonderful dexterity, fluency in (languages etc.), unrestricted, unrestrained

---

• この報道カメラマンは、世界中を自由自在に飛び回って活躍している。

Kono hōdō-kameraman wa, sekai-jū o jiyū-jizai ni tobimawatte katsuyaku shite iru.

This photojournalist flies round the world wherever he pleases, shooting assignments.

• 子供たちは自由自在に壁を塗り始めた。

Kodomo-tachi wa jiyū-jizai ni kabe o nurihajimeta.

The children began painting the wall in any way that struck their fancy.

• 首謀者は、手下を自由自在に操って、次々と犯罪を犯していった。

Shubō-sha wa, teshita o jiyū-jizai ni ayatsutte, tsugitsugi to hanzai o okashite itta.

Manipulating his henchmen as freely as puppets on a string, the ringleader went on to commit one crime after another.

● 彼は自由自在にはさみを使って、あっと言う間に複雑な切り絵を完成させた。

Kare wa jiyū-jizai ni hasami o tsukatte, atto iu ma ni fukuzatsu na kirie o kansei saseta.

Using the scissors as if they were a part of his own hand, he completed a complex cutout in no time at all.

縦横無尽 *jūō-mujin*

the length and breadth, inexhaustible

freely, in all directions, vigorously, tirelessly

● ひび割れが、壁中に縦横無尽に走っている。

Hibiware ga, kabejū ni jūō-mujin ni hashitte iru.

The wall is just a maze of cracks from top to bottom.

● この本の中で、著者はわが国の土地政策について縦横無尽に語っている。

Kono hon no naka de, chosha wa wagakuni no tochi-seisaku ni tsuite jūō-mujin ni katatte iru.

In this book the author expresses his far-reaching opinions about our national land policy.

● 今回のイベントでは、彼の縦横無尽な活躍ぶりが目立った。

Konkai no ibento de wa, kare no jūō-mujin na katsuyaku-buri ga medatta.

His tireless efforts on behalf of the event this time were quite remarkable.

十人十色 *jūnin-toiro*

ten people, ten colors

so many men, so many minds; one man's meat is another man's poison; it takes all kinds (to make a world)

• みんなの意見は十人十色で、とてもまとまりそうにないよ。

Minna no iken wa jūnin-toiro de, totemo matomarisō ni nai yo.

With everyone being of a different mind, it's unlikely we'll be able to wrap this one up smoothly.

• 異性の好みは十人十色で、だから世の中うまくいくのかな。

Isei no konomi wa jūnin-toiro de, dakara yo no naka umaku iku no ka na.

About the opposite sex, there are as many different tastes as there are people; maybe that's what makes the world go round.

➔ 三人三様 (*sannin-san'yō*) or 三者三様 (*sansha-san'yō*)—literally, three people, three ways—are synonymous expressions, though the numbers involved are different.

受験地獄 *juken-jigoku*

examination hell

the intense competition among Japanese students for acceptance at junior high schools, high schools, and universities

---

• 女房は、子供に受験地獄を経験させたくないからって、エスカレーター式の有名幼稚園に入れようとしてるんだ。

Nyōbō wa, kodomo ni juken-jigoku o keiken sasetaku nai kara tte, esukarētā-shiki no yūmei-yōchien ni ireyō to shite 'ru n' da.

My wife says she doesn't want to put our kids through the gruelling experience of preparing for secondary school and college exams, so she's trying to get them into a famous kindergarten where they can get a free pass into its affiliated schools.

- 大学受験が、受験地獄とか受験戦争とか呼ばれるようになったのは、いつごろからだろうか。

Daigaku-juken ga, juken-jigoku to ka juken-sensō to ka yobareru yō ni natta no wa, itsugoro kara darō ka.

I wonder when studying for university entrance exams came to be known as "exam hell" and "exam war."

取捨選択 *shusha-sentaku*
selecting and choosing
selection or rejection, choice

- 大掃除のときはいつも、何を捨てるかの取捨選択に丸一日かかってしまうんだ。

Ōsōji no toki wa itsumo, nani o suteru ka no shusha-sentaku ni maru-ichinichi kakatte shimau n' da.

Every time I do spring-cleaning, I end up spending the whole day deciding what to keep and what to throw away.

- 手当たり次第にやってみるのも一つのやり方だと思うけど、ある程度は取捨選択した方がいいよ。

Teatari-shidai ni yatte miru no mo hitotsu no yarikata da to omou kedo, aru teido wa shusha-sentaku shita hō ga ii yo.

Doing whatever comes to hand is one way of doing things, but you really ought to pick and choose a bit.

純真無垢 *junshin-muku*
pure and clean
innocent, as pure as the driven snow

• 彼女の純真無垢な心に触れて、私のすさんでいた心も洗わ
れたような気がする。

*Kanojo no junshin-muku na kokoro ni furete, watashi no su-
sande ita kokoro mo arawareta yō na ki ga suru.*

Meeting somebody as pure and innocent as her makes me feel
as though I've been made whole again.

• 彼は純真無垢で、思ったことを素直に言ってるだけなんだ
が、生意気だと誤解されていじめられているみたいだ。

*Kare wa junshin-muku de, omotta koto o sunao ni itte 'ru dake
nan da ga, namaiki da to gokai sarete ijimerarete iru mitai
da.*

He simply says what he thinks in all innocence, but they take it
as impertinence and pick on him.

順風満帆 *junpū-manpan*
sails full of a favorable wind
with the wind in one's sails, swimmingly, full steam
ahead, (smooth sailing) with the wind at one's back

• 子役として人気が出て以来、順風満帆の女優人生を歩んで
きた。

*Koyaku toshite ninki ga dete irai, junpū-manpan no joyū-jinsei
o ayunde kita.*

Since coming to popularity while still a child, she has sailed
through life as a successful actress.

• これまでは必ずしも順風満帆じゃなかったけど、やっと俺
にも運が向いてきたらしい。

*Kore made wa kanarazushimo junpū-manpan ja nakatta kedo,
yatto ore ni mo un ga muite kita rashii.*

Things haven't always gone smoothly up until now, but at last
my luck seems to have taken a turn for the better.

情状酌量 *jōjō-shakuryō*

circumstances (taken into) consideration

taking mitigating circumstances into consideration when dealing with an offender; clemency, leniency

---

- これだけの事件を起こしたんだ。情状酌量の余地はないよ。

Kore dake no jiken o okoshita n' da. Jōjō-shakuryō no yochi wa nai yo.

There can be no room for clemency in a case such as this (as big as this).

- 弁護士は被告人の不幸な生い立ちを述べて、情状酌量を訴えた。

Bengo-shi wa hikoku-nin no fukō na oitachi o nobete, jōjō-shakuryō o uttaeta.

The lawyer spoke of the defendant's unhappy childhood, and pleaded for clemency.

- 今日で今週3回目の遅刻だぞ！　もう情状酌量の余地はないな。

Kyō de konshū sankai-me no chikoku da zo! Mō jōjō-shakuryō no yochi wa nai na.

Today is the third time you've been late this week! Don't expect to be let off lightly.

正真正銘 *shōshin-shōmei*

genuine article, authentic signature

the real McCoy, the genuine article, authentic, the real thing

---

- 「スコッチウイスキー」は山ほどあるが、正真正銘のものは少ない。

"Sukotchi uisukī" wa yama hodo aru ga, shōshin-shōmei no mono wa sukunai.

There are plenty of "Scotch" whiskies around, but very few of them are the real McCoy.

• これは間違いなく、正真正銘のダリですよ。

Kore wa machigai naku, shōshin-shōmei no Dari desu yo.

Without any doubt, this is a genuine Dali.

小心翼々 ***shōshin-yokuyoku***

small heart, many feathers

cowardly, faint-hearted, (over-)cautious, timid, spineless, wimpish, weak-kneed, namby-pamby

• そんな小心翼々としたことでどうするんだ。もっと堂々としてなさい。

Sonna shōshin-yokuyoku to shita koto de dō suru n' da. Motto dōdō to shite inasai.

Why are you acting as though you're afraid of your own shadow? Let's see a little more backbone!

• あいつ意外と小心翼々としてるんだよな、今度のことでよく分かったよ。

Aitsu igai to shōshin-yokuyoku to shite 'ru n' da yo na, kondo no koto de yoku wakatta yo.

I just realized it from what happened the other day, but he's a surprisingly timid guy.

→ Originally this expression was used to mean "scrupulously and with great attention to detail," but in later years it came to take on the pejorative meanings listed above.

少数精鋭 *shōsū-seiei*

small number, sharp spirits

an elite corps; a select few; the cream of the crop; the creme de la creme

---

• もう人海戦術は古い。これからは少数精鋭主義で行かなくちゃ。

Mō jinkai-senjutsu wa furui. Kore kara wa shōsū-seiei-shugi de ikanakucha.

Trying to solve problems by throwing more and more people into the fray is out-of-date. From now on we've got to slim down our operation and make ourselves into an elite corps.

• この部隊は、自衛隊きっての少数精鋭、つまりエリート部隊なんだ。

Kono butai wa, jiei-tai kitte no shōsū-seiei, tsumari erīto-butai nan da.

This unit is the Self-Defense Force's crack outfit. They are, in other words, the elite troops.

少壮気鋭 *shōsō-kiei*

young and sharp-spirited

young and enthusiastic, up-and-coming, young and energetic, full of youthful talent and spirit, young and keen, young and full of vim and vigor, a bright-faced go-getter

---

• 林教授は少壮気鋭の学者だ。

Hayashi-kyōju wa shōsō-kiei no gakusha da.

Professor Hayashi is a gifted young scholar (an up-and-coming scholar full of talent).

• こちらが少壮気鋭の翻訳家、滝本さんです。

Kochira ga shōsō-kiei no hon'yaku-ka, Takimoto-san desu.

May I introduce Mr. Takimoto, an up-and-coming translator worth watching out for.

→ The expression 新進気鋭 (*shinshin-kiei*) is virtually synonymous. While 少壮気鋭 is used to describe people in their twenties and thirties who are full of dynamism and pep, 新進気鋭 is used to describe people who are new on the scene or new to a certain field of activity. People entering into new fields of endeavor are generally young (especially, in Japan), so the two expressions are virtually synonymous. However, if (for example) you were talking about an office worker in his fifties who had quit his job and become a successful writer, you could only use 新進気鋭.

商売繁盛 *shōbai-hanjō*
business is flourishing
business is booming, business is on the up and up, doing a roaring trade, doing good business

---

• ご商売繁盛で結構ですねえ。

Go-shōbai-hanjō de kekkō desu nē.

So business is booming. That's nice.

• はごいた市は、商売繁盛を願って縁起物の羽子板を買いに来た人たちで一杯だ。

Hagoita-ichi wa, shōbai-hanjō o negatte engi-mono no hagoita o kai ni kita hito-tachi de ippai da.

The battledore market is full of people who have come to buy battledore charms to bring prosperity to their business.

❑ 羽子板 (*hagoita*) is a wooden bat (a bit larger than a tabletennis paddle in size) on which a picture is usually painted. At New Year children traditionally play *hanetsuki*, a game not dissimilar to badminton, using the bats and a *hane* (a kind of shuttlecock). In addition, many people buy the bats as talismans (*engi-mono*) which they hang up on the walls of their home. It is this custom that is being alluded to in the above example.

● この神社は商売繁盛の神様をまつっているんだよ。

Kono jinja wa shōbai-hanjō no kamisama o matsutte iru n' da yo.

This shrine is dedicated to the god of prosperous business.

枝葉末節 *shiyō-massetsu*
branch, leaves, end joints
trivial details, unimportant details, trifling details,
trifles, matters of extremely minor importance

● 君は枝葉末節にこだわり過ぎるよ。もっと大きな視点から、物事を見られないかね。

Kimi wa shiyō-massetsu ni kodawarisugiru yo. Motto ōkina shiten kara, monogoto o mirarenai ka ne.

You pay too much attention to trivial details. You're gonna have to start seeing things as part of a bigger picture.

● 枝葉末節にとらわれていると、大切なことを見逃してしまうよ。

Shiyō-massetsu ni torawarete iru to, taisetsu na koto o minogashite shimau yo.

If you let yourself get caught up in trifling details, you'll end up missing what's important.

職人気質 *shokunin-katagi* or *shokunin-kishitsu*
the artisan spirit
craftsmanship, attention and devotion to quality

• 昔のような職人気質の大工さんは、このごろでは見られなくなったね。

Mukashi no yō na shokunin-katagi (shokunin-kishitsu) no daiku-san wa, konogoro de wa mirarenaku natta ne.

Nowadays you no longer see carpenters who are really devoted to their craft the way they used to be.

• いろんな物が機械で大量生産されている時代だからこそ、職人気質を忘れないで、手作りにこだわりたいんですよ。

Ironna mono ga kikai de tairyō-seisan sarete iru jidai da kara koso, shokunin-katagi (shokunin-kishitsu) o wasurenai de, tezukuri ni kodawaritai n' desu yo.

It's precisely because we're living in an age when all sorts of things are mass-produced by machines that I want to stick to handicrafts and keep alive the artisan spirit.

植物人間 *shokubutsu-ningen*
vegetable human being
a (human) vegetable

• 妻が手術中の事故で植物人間になってしまったので、夫は病院と医師を訴えた。

Tsuma ga shujutsu-chū no jiko de shokubutsu-ningen ni natte shimatta no de, otto wa byōin to ishi o uttaeta.

His wife ended up a vegetable as a result of a botched operation, so he sued the hospital and the surgeon responsible.

• もしも私が植物人間になったら、延命治療はしないでほしい。

Moshimo watashi ga shokubutsu-ningen ni nattara, enmei-chiryō wa shinai de hoshii.

If I should ever end up a human vegetable, I don't want to receive treatment to prolong my life.

私利私欲 *shiri-shiyoku*

one's own interests, one's own desires

self-interest, personal gain, feathering one's own nest, lining one's own pockets

• 残念ながら、わが国の政治家には国民のためというより、私利私欲のために行動している人が多い。

Zannen nagara, wagakuni no seiji-ka ni wa kokumin no tame to iu yori, shiri-shiyoku no tame ni kōdō shite iru hito ga ōi.

Sadly, most politicians in this country are more intent on feathering their own nests than working on behalf of the people.

• 私利私欲に駆られて、他人をけおとしてきた自分が、今ではむなしいよ。

Shiri-shiyoku ni kararete, tanin o keotoshite kita jibun ga, ima de wa munashii yo.

Driven by blind self-interest, I've gotten ahead by pushing others aside. What a wasted life it's been.

支離滅裂 *shiri-metsuretsu*

support (taken) away (leads to) ruin and destruction

incoherence, inconsistency, disruption, chaos, utter confusion, gobbledegook

• まだ熱が高くて、言うことも支離滅裂なんだよ。

Mada netsu ga takakute, iu koto mo shiri-metsuretsu nan da yo.

He's still running a high temperature and is making no sense whatsoever (you can't make out a word of what he's saying).

• こんな支離滅裂なことを書いて来て、どういうつもりかね。

Konna shiri-metsuretsu na koto o kaite kite, dō iu tsumori ka ne.

What do you mean by bringing me this incoherent mess?

人海戦術 *jinkai-senjutsu*

a human-sea strategy

adopt human wave tactics, send in a sea of bodies (to deal with a problem or a situation)

• もう時間がない！原始的だが全員集めて人海戦術で行こう。

Mō jikan ga nai! Genshi-teki da ga zen'in atsumete jinkai-senjutsu de ikō.

We're running out of time. It's primitive, I know, but let's get everybody together and throw them into the fray.

この国は、人海戦術を駆使して、短期間のうちに経済発展を遂げた。

Kono kuni wa, jinkai-senjutsu o kushi shite, tan-jikan no uchi ni keizai-hatten o togeta.

This country mobilized its people and through sheer weight of numbers made incredible economic progress in a very short time.

心機一転 *shinki-itten*

a complete change of heart

a change of mind, a change of heart, turning over a new leaf, making a fresh start in life, taking a new lease on life

---

• 入院をきっかけに心機一転し、体をもっと大切にしようと決心した。

Nyūin o kikkake ni shinki-itten shi, karada o motto taisetsu ni shiyō to kesshin shita.

Being hospitalized really changed me (gave me a new perspective on life). I've decided to be a lot more careful about my health.

● 彼女は香港への転勤で心機一転、人生の再出発を決意した。

Kanojo wa Honkon e no tenkin de shinki-itten, jinsei no sai-shuppatsu o ketsui shita.

She saw her transfer to Hong Kong as an ideal chance to turn over a new leaf and make a fresh start in life.

神出鬼没 *shinshutsu-kibotsu*

god comes out, the devil sinks (disappears)

elusive, (as) slippery (as an eel); here one minute, gone the next; (gone) like a ghost in the night

---

● さっきまでここにいたのに、まったく彼は神出鬼没だね。

Sakki made koko ni ita no ni, mattaku kare wa shinshutsu-kibotsu da ne.

He was here just a second ago. That's just like him—here one minute, gone the next.

● 神出鬼没の泥棒は、必死の捜査にもかかわらずなかなか捕まらない。

Shinshutsu-kibotsu no dorobō wa, hisshi no sōsa ni mo kakawarazu nakanaka tsukamaranai.

In spite of an exhaustive manhunt by the police, the burglar has managed to slip like a phantom through their fingers.

針小棒大 *shinshō-bōdai*

(to make something) as small as a needle as big as a stick

making a mountain out of a molehill; exaggerating

- 彼女はいつも物事を針小棒大に言うから、少し割引きして
  聞いたほうがいいよ。

*Kanojo wa itsumo monogoto o shinshō-bōdai ni iu kara,
sukoshi waribiki shite kiita hō ga ii yo.*

She always makes a mountain out of a molehill, so I'd take it
all with a pinch of salt if I were you.

- スポーツ新聞の見出しは針小棒大のことが多くて、見出し
  にひかれて買ってしまってから後悔する。

*Supōtsu-shinbun no midashi wa shinshō-bōdai no koto ga
ōkute, midashi ni hikarete katte shimatte kara kōkai suru.*

The headlines in sports newspapers are often wildly sensa-
tional. Your eye gets caught by these headlines, but after
you've bought the paper you regret it.

新進気鋭 *shinshin-kiei*

new and sharp

up-and-coming; someone to watch

- 君のような新進気鋭の医者に来てもらえれば、うちの病院
  も鬼に金棒だよ。

*Kimi no yō na shinshin-kiei no isha ni kite moraereba, uchi no
byōin mo oni ni kanabō da yo.*

If we could get an up-and-coming doctor such as yourself to
work at our hospital, we would make an unbeatable team.

- これは、この間賞をとった新進気鋭の作家の作品ですね。

*Kore wa, kono aida shō o totta shinshin-kiei no sakka no
sakuhin desu ne.*

This is a book by that up-and-coming writer who won that
award the other day.

深慮遠謀 *shinryo-enbō*
thoughtfulness and foresight
carefully laid plans for the future; farsighted; meticulous in one's planning

---

- 今回の作戦は、彼の深慮遠謀の結果だった。

Konkai no sakusen wa, kare no shinryo-enbō no kekka datta.

Our strategy this time is the result of his meticulous planning.

- あいつは行きあたりばったりで、深慮遠謀には縁がない。

Aitsu wa yukiatari-battari de, shinryo-enbō ni wa en ga nai.

Always leaving things to chance the way he does, he can
   hardly be called meticulous in his planning.

- 自分は決して表に出ないのが、この政治家の深慮遠謀だよ。

*Jibun wa kesshite omote ni denai no ga, kono seiji-ka no shin-
   ryo-enbō da yo.*

That politician always carefully plans it so that he stays well
   out of the public eye.

→ The phrase can also be written as 深謀遠慮 (*shinbō-enryo*); here the
meaning of *enryo* is not "to refrain from doing something," but "to
look to the future."

頭寒足熱 *zukan-sokunetsu*
a cold head and warm feet
keeping the head cool and the feet warm

- 昔から頭寒足熱は健康に良いとされてるね。

*Mukashi kara zukan-sokunetsu wa kenkō ni yoi to sarete 'ru
   ne.*

It's always been said that keeping your feet warm and your
   head cool is good for the health.

• 部屋中こんなに暑くしてちゃ、頭がのぼせるよ。頭寒足熱を心がけなくちゃ。

Heya-jū konna ni atsuku shite 'cha, atama ga noboseru yo. Zukan-sokunetsu o kokorogakenakucha.

If you keep your room as hot as this, the blood will rush to your head. Keeping your feet warm but your head cool is the way to do it.

❑ This four-character compound contains a traditional piece of Japanese folk wisdom that is of particular cultural interest. By keeping the air temperature in a room quite low (by letting the outside fresh air in), we are less prone to catching colds (as germs thrive in a warm, stuffy environment), and we are better able to keep a cool head and think clearly. However, if we don't keep our feet warm, we feel crotchety and bad-tempered. How do the Japanese maintain this healthy equilibrium between a cool head and warm feet? Simple. They invented the *kotatsu*, a low square table covered with a quilt, under which a small electric heater is placed (before the days of electricity, charcoal was used). You sit on the floor with your legs under the quilt, and your feet stay nice and warm.

誠心誠意 *seishin-seii*
sincere mind, sincere intention
sincerely, faithfully, wholeheartedly

• 採用していただければ、誠心誠意会社のために働きます。

Saiyō shite itadakereba, seishin-seii kaisha no tame ni hatara-kimasu.

If you hire me, I will be a faithful and devoted employee.

• 説得しようと誠心誠意話してみたが、とりつく島もなかったよ。

Settoku shiyō to seishin-seii hanashite mita ga, toritsuku shima mo nakatta yo.

I tried with the best will in the world to persuade him, but I just couldn't get through.

● 彼の誠心誠意の態度には、打たれますね。

Kare no seishin-seii no taido ni wa, utaremasu ne.

I'm really impressed by his sincere attitude.

正々堂々 *seisei-dōdō*

true and noble

fair and square; open and aboveboard; on the level; openly and fairly

---

● 正々堂々と胸を張った生き方がしたいんです。

Seisei-dōdō to mune o hatta ikikata ga shitai n' desu.

I want to live life fair and square, with my head held high.

● 自分にやましいところがないなら、もっと正々堂々としていなさい。

Jibun ni yamashii tokoro ga nai nara, motto seisei-dōdō to shite inasai.

If you've got nothing to be ashamed of, then stop acting as if you've got something to hide.

● 意見があるなら、陰口じゃなくて正々堂々と会議の場で言いたまえ。

Iken ga aru nara, kageguchi ja nakute seisei-dōdō to kaigi no ba de iitamae.

Don't talk behind people's backs. If you've got something to say, say it loud and clear at a meeting.

贅沢三昧 *zeitaku-zanmai*

concentration on luxury

burn the candle at both ends, give oneself over to a life
of pleasure, sow one's wild oats, live for pleasure

- 若い頃、贅沢三昧の生活をした罰があたったんでしょうか。
年取ってからは苦労続きです。

*Wakai koro, zeitaku-zanmai no seikatsu o shita batsu ga atatta
n' deshō ka. Toshitotte kara wa kurō-tsuzuki desu.*

When I was young, I burned the candle at both ends, but it
seems I'm paying for it now. As I get on in years, I'm having nothing but trouble.

- ブランド物を買いあさって、贅沢三昧をしていたバブル全
盛の頃が懐かしいな。

*Burando-mono o kaisatte, zeitaku-zanmai o shite ita baburu-
zensei no koro ga natsukashii na.*

I miss the days of the bubble economy, buying designer goods
and indulging in every whim.

清廉潔白 *seiren-keppaku*

honest and pure

(a person of) integrity; (a person with) an unblemished
record; totally blameless, beyond reproach, as straight
as a die

- 私は賄賂なんかもらってない。清廉潔白だ。

Watashi wa wairo nanka moratte 'nai. Seiren-keppaku da.

There's no way I've taken any bribes. I'm as straight as a die.

- あの人のように誠実で清廉潔白な政治家はもう出て来ない
だろうな。

Ano hito no yō ni seijitsu de seiren-keppaku na seiji-ka wa mō dete konai darō na.

I don't suppose we'll ever see any politicians as honest and as upright as him again.

切磋琢磨 *sessa-takuma*

cut, plane, fashion, and polish

to strive to improve oneself intellectually or morally;
to strive together with others for such improvement

• 彼らはお互いに切磋琢磨するより、いかに相手に勝つかばかり考えているようだ。

Karera wa otagai ni sessa-takuma suru yori, ika ni aite ni katsu ka bakari kangaete iru yō da.

Instead of trying to learn from each other and improve themselves, all they seem to think about is how they can beat the other guy.

• 新入社員諸君は、この研修期間に切磋琢磨しあって、おおいに実力をつけてもらいたい。

Shinnyū-shain shokun wa, kono kenshū-kikan ni sessa-takuma shiatte, ōi ni jitsuryoku o tsukete moraitai.

What we want from all you new recruits during this induction period is for you to work hard together at developing your abilities.

❏ Just as in former times an artisan would cut (切), then file and plane (磋), then form the shape (琢), and finally polish (磨) a piece of ivory or horn to make a gorgeous piece of jewelry, so we too must work hard to improve ourselves.

絶体絶命 *zettai-zetsumei*

desperate body, desperate life

a desperate (critical) situation, a (tight) corner, a bad fix, a real bind, up the creek (without a paddle)

- 007は、何回も絶体絶命の危機に直面しながら、いつも助かることになっている。

Zero-zero-sebun wa, nankai mo zettai-zetsumei no kiki ni chokumen shinagara, itsumo tasukaru koto ni natte iru.

James Bond is forever getting into impossibly tight corners, but he always manages to get out of them again.

- もうごまかしはきかない。絶体絶命だ。横領がばれてしまった。

Mō gomakashi wa kikanai. Zettai-zetsumei da. Ōryō ga barete shimatta.

None of your excuses are going to work this time. You're in deep trouble. They've found out you've been cooking the books.

千客万来 *senkyaku-banrai*

a thousand customers (guests) coming ten thousand times

to have one visitor after another, to have an interminable succession of visitors, to be pulling in the crowds

- 今日は千客万来で、すごく忙しい。

Kyō wa senkyaku-banrai de, sugoku isogashii.

We've been rushed off our feet today with all the customers we've had.

• 千客万来の一日で、たまってた仕事が全然かたづかなかっ
たよ。

Senkyaku-banrai no ichinichi de, tamatte 'ta shigoto ga zenzen katazukanakatta yo.

I had so many visitors today that I couldn't get around to all the work that's piled up.

前後不覚 *zengo-fukaku*

before and after, no recollection

to be dead to the world, out for the count, in a stupor, to pass out

---

• ゆうべまた、調子にのって飲み過ぎて、前後不覚になった
らしい。何も覚えていないんだ。

Yūbe mata, chōshi ni notte nomisugite, zengo-fukaku ni natta rashii. Nani mo oboete inai n' da.

I got carried away again last night, drank myself silly, and apparently passed out. I don't remember a thing.

• 夕べは疲れていたので、前後不覚に10時間以上も寝てしま
った。

Yūbe wa tsukarete ita no de, zengo-fukaku ni jūji-kan ijō mo nete shimatta.

Last night I was so tired that I just conked out and slept for over ten hours.

千載一遇 *senzai-ichigū*

meeting once in a thousand years

once in a lifetime

• こんな千載一遇のチャンスを逃す手はないよ。

Konna senzai-ichigū no chansu o nogasu te wa nai yo.

There's no way you're going to let slip this chance of a lifetime.

● 千載一遇の投資の機会だと勧められて、話にのったのが間
違いだった。

*Senzai-ichigū no tōshi no kikai da to susumerarete, hanashi ni
notta no ga machigai datta.*

It was presented as the investment chance of a lifetime, so I
went along with it. Was that a mistake!

戦々恐々 *sensen-kyōkyō*

trembling and frightened

timidly, with fear and trembling, in great fear, ner-
vously, gingerly, on tenterhooks

● まだ余震が来るかも知れないので、戦々恐々の毎日ですよ。

*Mada yoshin ga kuru ka mo shirenai no de, sensen-kyōkyō no
mainichi desu yo.*

There's still a chance of after-shocks, so everyday we're on
tenterhooks.

● いつわが社にも捜査のメスが入るか、戦々恐々としている。

*Itsu wagasha ni mo sōsa no mesu ga hairu ka, sensen-kyōkyō
to shite iru.*

We are all practically quaking in our boots, wondering when
they are going to probe into our company, too.

前代未聞 *zendai-mimon*

never heard of before

unheard of, unprecedented, unparalleled (in history),
record-breaking, rare, unusual

• 宗教団体による、この前代未聞の犯罪には、日本中がショックを受けた。

Shūkyō-dantai ni yoru, kono zendai-mimon no hanzai ni wa, nihon-jū ga shokku o uketa.

Japan was shocked by the unprecedented scale of the crime committed by the religious cult.

• 役人が役所の内情を暴露した本を書くなんて、前代未聞だね。

Yakunin ga yakusho no naijō o bakuro shita hon o kaku nante, zendai-mimon da ne.

It's unheard of for a civil servant to write a book exposing the inner workings of the Japanese bureaucracy.

先手必勝 *sente-hisshō*
the first hand (is) sure to win
the player who makes the first move in a game is sure to win, to make the first strike, to seize the initiative, to take the game by the scruff of the neck

---

• このゲームは先手必勝だからね。とにかく攻めの一手だよ。

Kono gēmu wa sente-hisshō da kara ne. Tonikaku seme no itte da yo.

Whoever seizes the initiative in this game is going to win it. We've got to go out there and attack.

• 先手必勝で行こうと思ってはいたんだが、つい守りにまわってしまった。

Sente-hisshō de ikō to omotte wa ita n' da ga, tsui mamori ni mawatte shimatta.

We went out there determined to attack from the start, but before we knew it, we found ourselves pushed back on the defensive.

前途洋々 *zento-yōyō*

the road ahead is broad and wide

one's future prospects are good; the outlook is good; you've got a bright (promising) future before you; the future's looking good (rosy); the future's coming up roses

---

● 一流大学卒業、一流企業へ就職、とまさに前途洋々だねえ。

Ichiryū-daigaku sotsugyō, ichiryū-kigyō e shūshoku, to masa ni zento-yōyō da nē.

What with you graduating from a top university and now getting a job with a major company, your future's certainly looking rosy.

● 出世間違いなし、前途洋々の青年だって仲人さんが言ったから結婚したのに……。

Shusse machigai nashi, zento-yōyō no seinen datte nakōdo-san ga itta kara kekkon shita no ni ...

To think that I married him because the matchmaker said he was certain to get promoted, that he was a young man with a bright future ...

→ There is a four-character compound with the opposite meaning to this, which is 前途多難 (*zento-tanan*). Its literal meaning is "on the road ahead there are many difficulties." In more idiomatic English we might say someone "has got their work cut out for them" or "is in for a rough ride ahead." See the examples below.

● かえったばかりのカメの赤ちゃんはやっと海へ入っていった。でもまだまだこれから前途多難だ。

Kaetta bakari no kame no akachan wa yatto umi e haitte itta. Demo mada mada kore kara zento-tanan da.

The newly hatched baby turtles managed to make their way to the sea. But many many obstacles still lie ahead.

• 企画会議はなんとか通ったが、まだまだ前途多難だよ。

Kikaku-kaigi wa nan to ka tōta ga, mada mada zento-tanan da yo.

We managed to get our plan accepted by the project committee, but we're still facing an uphill struggle.

相思相愛 *sōshi-sōai*

think of each other, love each other

mutual love, reciprocal affection, to be in love with one another

---

• 相思相愛で結ばれたはずが、1年もしないうちに別れちゃった。

Sōshi-sōai de musubareta hazu ga, ichinen mo shinai uchi ni wakarechatta.

They were supposed to be madly in love, but within a year they'd split up.

• そのうち、あなたにも相思相愛の相手が現れるよ。

Sono uchi, anata ni mo sōshi-sōai no aite ga arawareru yo.

It won't be long before you too have someone of your own to love and cherish.

• あいつら相思相愛だからさあ、一緒にいるとあてられっぱなしだよ。

Aitsura sōshi-sōai da kara sā, issho ni iru to aterareppanashi da yo.

They're just a couple of lovebirds, and they're always flaunting it when you're with them.

大器晩成 *taiki-bansei*

great talents mature late

to achieve greatness late in life; great talents are slow in maturing; to be a late (slow) developer, a late bloomer; to bloom (hit one's peak) late in life

• この子のんびり屋でちょっと心配なんだけど、みんなは大器晩成だって言ってくれるのよ。

Kono ko nonbiri-ya de chotto shinpai nan da kedo, minna wa taiki-bansei datte itte kureru no yo.

Our kid's so laid back it worries me sometimes, but everyone tells me he's just a late developer.

• 大器晩成と言われ続けて、還暦を迎えてしまった。

Taiki-bansei to iwaretsuzukete, kanreki o mukaete shimatta.

All my life people have told me I'm a late developer, but here I am turning sixty!

大言壮語 *taigen-sōgo*

big talk, brave language

big (tall) talk, bragging, boasting, swaggering

• あんな大言壮語して、大丈夫なのかね。

Anna taigen-sōgo shite, daijōbu na no ka ne.

I wonder if he ought to bragging quite so much.

• 君の大言壮語は聞きあきたよ。そろそろ結果を見せてくれ。

Kimi no taigen-sōgo wa kikiakita yo. Sorosoro kekka o misete kure.

I'm fed up with you and your big mouth. How about showing us some results one of these days.

大根役者 *daikon-yakusha*

a radish actor

a ham actor, a lousy (poor) actor

• 若い頃「大根役者」と言われたのに奮起して、押しも押されもしない名優になった。

Wakai koro "daikon-yakusha" to iwareta no ni funki shite, oshi mo osare mo shinai meiyū ni natta.

Called "a ham actor" while young, he was inspired to become one of the best actors around.

• いくら顔が良くても、あんな大根役者じゃどうしようもないよ。

Ikura kao ga yokute mo, anna daikon-yakusha ja dō shiyō mo nai yo.

I don't care how handsome he is; the guy's still hopeless as an actor.

泰然自若 *taizen-jijaku*

calm and composed

imperturbable; with great presence of mind; cool, calm and collected; as cool as a cucumber; (to keep) a cool head; a model of composure

---

• ここまで来るともう覚悟ができたらしく、泰然自若としている。

Koko made kuru to mō kakugo ga dekita rashiku, taizen-jijaku to shite iru.

Having gotten this far, he seems prepared for anything; he's as cool as a cucumber.

• さっきまで泰然自若としていたが、急にそわそわし始めた。

Sakki made taizen-jijaku to shite ita ga, kyū ni sowasowa shi-hajimeta.

Up until a minute ago he was a model of composure, but all of a sudden he's begun to get on edge.

➡ The difference between 泰然自若 and 冷静沈着 (*reisei-chinchaku*), although they are similar, is that, first, the former is accompanied by to *shite iru* while the latter is followed by *na* or *da*; secondly, in terms of meaning the former suggests leisurely body movement (or action) as a result of mental composure; on the other hand, the latter doesn't necessarily entail any degree of leisureliness. Thus, 冷静沈着に素早く行動する (*Reisei-chinchaku ni subayaku kōdō suru*) (to act quickly and calmly) is possible, but you cannot use 泰然自若 here.

大胆不敵 *daitan-futeki*

bold and daring

audacious, daredevil, undaunted, intrepid, brave, as bold as brass, fearless; to not know the meaning of fear

---

• その武将は大胆不敵な人物だった。

Sono bushō wa daitan-futeki na jinbutsu datta.

The general was incredibly courageous and brave.

• 泥棒は大胆不敵にも正面玄関から出入りしたらしい。

Dorobō wa daitan-futeki ni mo shōmen-genkan kara deiri shita rashii.

The burglar was as bold as brass, apparently entering and exiting by the front door.

他人行儀 *tanin-gyōgi*

act as if you were strangers

stand on formality, stand on ceremony, act like a stranger

● そんな他人行儀なこと、おっしゃらないで下さいな。

Sonna tanin-gyōgi na koto, ossharanai de kudasai na.

Please don't stand on ceremony.

● 松井さんとは知り合ってもう何年にもなるのに、いつまで たっても他人行儀なんだ。

Matsui-san to wa shiriatte mō nan-nen ni mo naru no ni, itsu made tatte mo tanin-gyōgi nan da.

Even though I've known Matsui for years, he always stands on formality.

他力本願 *tariki-hongan*

fulfill one's wish depending on others' power

reliance upon others, to get others to do your work for you, to always turn to others for help

---

● あいつは他力本願でいけないな。自分では何もしないで、 いつも人を当てにしてる。

Aitsu wa tariki-hongan de ikenai na. Jibun de wa nani mo shinai de, itsumo hito o ate ni shite 'ru.

He'll never get anywhere, always relying on others and never doing anything himself.

● 会社の危機なのに上層部は他力本願で、互いに誰かがなん とかしてくれるのを期待している様子だ。

Kaisha no kiki na no ni jōsō-bu wa tariki-hongan de, tagai ni dare ka ga nan to ka shite kureru no o kitai shite iru yōsu da.

Even though the company's in a crisis, the upper echelons all seem to be hoping that somebody will come along and save the situation, without doing anything themselves.

❏ This four-character compound is originally a Buddhist term meaning "salvation by faith through the benevolence of Amida

Buddha." It is the Buddhist belief that your deeds in this life will determine what you become in your next life (when you are reincarnated). If you are noble and honest, perhaps you will return as an eagle. If not, perhaps you will return as a rat. The process of reincarnation itself, however, is seen as a painful cycle of birth and death, from which it is difficult to escape. There are two ways to achieve one's 本願 (the desire to break out of the reincarnation cycle and attain eternal bliss, being reborn on a lotus leaf in Buddhist heaven): the first, called 他力本願 (*tariki-hongan*), is by putting oneself in Buddha's hands. The second, called 自力本願 (*jiriki-hongan*), meaning "trying to seek salvation relying on one's own strength," is by practising asceticism.

単純明快 *tanjun-meikai*

simple and clear

as clear as day, plain and simple, pellucid

• これほど単純明快な話はないよ。

Kore hodo tanjun-meikai na hanashi wa nai yo.

There couldn't be anything simpler than this.

• こんな単純明快な理屈も分からないのかい？

Konna tanjun-meikai na rikutsu mo wakaranai no kai?

Can't you follow a line of reasoning as clear and as simple as that?

単身赴任 *tanshin-funin*

a solitary posting

going to a new post by oneself (without one's spouse and children)

• 単身赴任も長くなると、問題が多くなるらしいね。

Tanshin-funin mo nagaku naru to, mondai ga ōku naru rashii ne.

It seems the longer a post keeps you away from home and loved ones, the more problems arise.

● 父は京都へ単身赴任中だが、週末には必ず帰ってくるよ。

Chichi wa Kyōto e tanshin-funin-chū da ga, shūmatsu ni wa kanarazu kaette kuru yo.

Dad's away in Kyoto where he's been posted by his company, but he always comes home on weekends.

❏ This refers to a company posting where an employee (usually a man) is sent to work far away from home, and decides to go alone so as not to disrupt his children's education.

男尊女卑 *danson-johi*
men respected, women despised
the custom of treating women as inferior to men; male chauvinism

---

● 表向きは男女平等なんて言ってても、大企業ほど本音は男尊女卑なんだから。

Omotemuki wa danjo-byōdō nante itte 'te mo, dai-kigyō hodo honne wa danson-johi nan da kara.

Although in public they like to talk about sexual equality, in truth big corporations are deeply chauvinistic.

● 今時そんな男尊女卑の考え方をしてたら、結婚してくれる女性なんかいないよ。

Imadoki sonna danson-johi no kangaekata o shite 'tara, kekkon shite kureru josei nanka inai yo.

With a chauvinistic attitude like yours, you'll never find a woman to marry you in this day and age.

単刀直入 *tantō-chokunyū*

(with) a single sword (charge) straight in

without preamble, without mincing words, without beating about the bush, bluntly, directly, frankly

---

• 単刀直入に言うと、君はこの仕事には適性がないんだ。

Tantō-chokunyū ni iu to, kimi wa kono shigoto ni wa tekisei ga nai n' da.

To be perfectly frank with you, you're simply not cut out for this job.

• 失礼ながら、単刀直入におうかがいしますが、業績が上がる見通しがあるのですか。

Shitsurei nagara, tantō-chokunyū ni oukagai shimasu ga, gyōseki ga agaru mitōshi ga aru no desu ka.

Excuse me for asking quite so bluntly, but are there any prospects of your business improving?

中途半端 *chūto-hanpa*

halfway and incomplete

half-finished, half-done, half-hearted, incomplete, half-baked

---

• あいつは口だけは達者だけど、やることは中途半端なんだ。

Aitsu wa kuchi dake wa tassha da kedo, yaru koto wa chūto-hanpa nan da.

He talks up a storm, but he botches up everything he does.

• いつまでも中途半端な態度だと、彼女に振られちゃうよ。

Itsu made mo chūto-hanpa na taido da to, kanojo ni furare-chau yo.

If you don't start treating her a bit more seriously, she'll leave you, you know.

- こんな中途半端なやり方じゃ、効果が上がらないのは目に
  見えてるよ。

*Konna chūto-hanpa na yarikata ja, kōka ga agaranai no wa
me ni miete 'ru yo.*

It should be obvious to anybody that this half-baked way of
doing things is not going to produce results.

- 「中途半端は何もしないのと同じ」と上司に怒鳴られた。

*"Chūto-hanpa wa nani mo shinai to onaji" to jōshi ni dona-
rareta.*

The boss bawled me out, saying, "Doing only half a job is the
same as doing nothing at all."

昼夜兼行 *chūya-kenkō*
going both day and night
(work) day and night, flat out, around the clock

- 締切が迫って来たので、昼夜兼行で原稿を書いています。

*Shimekiri ga sematte kita no de, chūya-kenkō de genkō o kaite
imasu.*

With the deadline for my book approaching, I'm writing day
and night.

- このままじゃ納期に間に合わないぞ、今日から工場は昼夜
  兼行だ。

*Kono mama ja nōki ni ma ni awanai zo, kyō kara kōjō wa
chūya-kenkō da.*

At this rate we'll never make the delivery on time, so starting
today the factory's going on a 24-hour shift.

→ For another four-character compound with the same meaning, cf.
不眠不休 (*fumin-fukyū*).

亭主関白 *teishu-kanpaku*

husband and Chief Adviser to the Emperor

a tyrant in his own home, a despotic husband, a husband who lords it over his wife

---

- 彼は会社じゃおとなしいけど、家じゃすごい亭主関白らしいよ。

Kare wa kaisha ja otonashii kedo, uchi ja sugoi teishu-kanpaku rashii yo.

At the office he's as quiet as a mouse, but at home he's a right little Hitler, it seems.

- うちは蚤の夫婦だから、かかあ天下に見えるけど、実は亭主関白なの。

Uchi wa nomi no fūfu da kara, kakā-denka ni mieru kedo, jitsu wa teishu-kanpaku na no.

I'm much bigger than my husband, so people often think I wear the pants at home. In fact, it's him who's the boss.

→ かかあ天下 (*kakā-denka*) refers to a wife who wears the pants in the family.

☐ 蚤の夫婦 (*nomi no fūfu*) refers to a married couple where the wife is big and fat, and the husband small and thin. In Japanese it is "Mr. and Mrs. Flea," while in English we might say "Jack Sprat and his wife."

適材適所 *tekizai-tekisho*

the appropriate material (in) the appropriate place

the right person in the right place; the right person for the right job; just the person we need; just the ticket; well suited for the job (role)

• 適材適所と言いながら、実は情実人事が横行している。

Tekizai-tekisho to iinagara, jitsu wa jōjitsu-jinji ga ōkō shite iru.

They're always talking about choosing the best man for the job, but the fact is that favoritism rules the day.

• 優秀な人材を適材適所で使っていかなければ駄目だよ。

Yūshū na jinzai o tekizai-tekisho de tsukatte ikanakereba dame da yo.

You've got to use the best people you have effectively, putting the right people in the right places.

• 年功序列にこだわらず、適材適所の精神で、若い人をどんどん活用していきたいんだ。

Nenkō-joretsu ni kodawarazu, tekizai-tekisho no seishin de, wakai hito o dondon katsuyō shite ikitai n' da.

We want to make full use of our younger staff, putting them in jobs best suited to their abilities, without worrying about questions of seniority.

天衣無縫 *ten'i-muhō*

heavenly garments without a stitch (showing)

perfect, flawless; (a person of) artless and unaffected character; without artifice (airs and graces)

• この書家の天衣無縫な作風は誰にも真似が出来ない。

Kono shoka no ten'i-muhō na sakufū wa dare ni mo mane ga dekinai.

Nobody could possibly emulate this calligrapher's free and easy style.

• 彼は天才肌の優秀な男だが、天衣無縫過ぎたのが裏目に出た。

Kare wa tensai-hada no yūshū na otoko da ga, ten'i-muhō sugita no ga urame ni deta.

He is touched with genius, but his lack of guile has turned to his disadvantage.

❏ The literal meaning of 天衣無縫 is that angels' clothes show no trace of human handicraft (of having been sewn by the human hand). Their garments are so immaculate, there isn't a stitch showing. From this came the figurative meaning of something being very natural and beautiful, and it was often used to describe poetry or prose that was of impeccable style. Nowadays this meaning is no longer current; instead 天衣無縫 is now used as a synonym for 天真爛漫 (*tenshin-ranman*; see below); it is used to describe someone who doesn't worry too much about what other people think, who says what he thinks and does what he wants, but who has no malice in him and so is usually not thought ill of.

天下一品 *tenka-ippin*

only one under the sky

be unrivalled, second to none, be tops, be out of this world

• うちの兄貴のスピーチは天下一品だよ。どこであんなに上手になったんだろう。

Uchi no aniki no supīchi wa tenka-ippin da yo. Doko de anna ni jōzu ni natta n' darō.

My big brother's speeches are really something else. I wonder where he got to be so good.

• 玲子さんのお料理は天下一品ね。

Reiko-san no oryōri wa tenka-ippin ne.

Reiko's cooking is really out of this world.

天真爛漫 *tenshin-ranman*

heavenly purity overflowing

naivety, simplicity, innocence

- 天真爛漫な子供の笑顔を見ていると、嫌なことも忘れられます。

Tenshin-ranman na kodomo no egao o mite iru to, iya na koto mo wasureraremasu.

Just seeing a child's innocent smiling face makes us forget all the bad in the world.

- うちのおばあちゃんはまるで子供のように天真爛漫で、誰にでも好かれるんだ。

Uchi no obāchan wa marude kodomo no yō ni tenshin-ranman de, dare ni de mo sukareru n' da.

My grandmother has a child's innocent naivety and is loved by everyone.

- 監督の天真爛漫な人柄のせいでチームの人気はうなぎ上りだ。

Kantoku no tenshin-ranman na hitogara no sei de chīmu no ninki wa unaginobori da.

Thanks to our manager's open, forthright nature, our team's popularity is sky-rocketing.

独身貴族 *dokushin-kizoku*

single aristocrats

single people who can live very comfortably as they have no spouse to support (or live with their parents); footloose and fancy-free single people

---

- 独身貴族の生活が楽しめるのも今のうちだよ。せいぜい遊んでおきなさい。

Dokushin-kizoku no seikatsu ga tanoshimeru no mo ima no uchi da yo. Seizei asonde okinasai.

Now's the time to enjoy your bachelor status, so get out there and have some fun (sow some wild oats) while you can!

• 家の息子は、独身貴族っていうんでしょうかねえ、優雅で気ままな暮らしをしてますよ。

Uchi no musuko wa, dokushin-kizoku tte iu n' deshō ka nē, yūga de kimama na kurashi o shite 'masu yo.

I suppose that's what they call being young, free, and single. Our son's certainly enjoying the nice things of life, doing exactly as he pleases.

• 礼子さんの今度のマンションすごいわよ。やっぱり独身貴族は違うわね。

Reiko-san no kondo no manshon sugoi wa yo. Yappari dokushin-kizoku wa chigau wa ne.

Reiko's new apartment is really something. Things are certainly different when you're single and have money to spare.

独立独歩 *dokuritsu-doppo*

standing by oneself, walking by oneself

independence, self-reliance, standing on one's own two feet

• 子供たちには、まず独立独歩の精神を身につけさせたいと思っているんです。

Kodomo-tachi ni wa, mazu dokuritsu-doppo no seishin o mi ni tsukesasetai to omotte iru n' desu.

Above all I want to instill in my children a spirit of independence.

• 独立独歩の道を歩むべく、このたび脱サラする決心をいたしました。

Dokuritsu-doppo no michi o ayumu beku, kono tabi datsusara suru kesshin o itashimashita.

I have decided to quit the company because I feel I must branch out and stand on my own two feet.

二重人格 *nijū-jinkaku*

a double personality

a split personality, a double (dual) personality, a Jekyll and Hyde

---

- 彼の場合は、内弁慶なんて生やさしいものじゃない。完全な二重人格だ。

Kare no bāi wa, uchi-benkei nante nama-yasashii mono ja nai. Kanzen na nijū-jinkaku da.

It's not just that he's difficult (a handful) at home but as good as gold elsewhere. He's a downright Jekyll and Hyde.

- この本の著者によると、凶悪犯罪の犯人には二重人格者が多いらしい。

Kono hon no chosha ni yoru to, kyōaku-hanzai no hannin ni wa nijū-jinkaku-sha ga ōi rashii.

According to the author of this book, many criminals who commit violent crimes seem to have split personalities.

- 二重人格どころか、多重人格という症例もあるそうだ。

Nijū-jinkaku dokoro ka, tajū-jinkaku to iu shōrei mo aru sō da.

They say there are cases where the personality is not simply dual but actually multiple.

二束三文 *nisoku-sanmon*

two bundles for three mon

dirt cheap, at bargain-basement prices, for peanuts, for a song, for chicken feed, for next to nothing

---

- 売り急いでいたので、やむをえず二束三文で処分した。

Uriisoide ita no de, yamu o ezu nisoku-sanmon de shobun shita.

I was in a rush to sell, which unavoidably meant I got rid of them dirt cheap (at throwaway prices).

● 思い出の品だったが、二束三文にしかならなかった。

Omoide no shina datta ga, nisoku-sanmon ni shika naranakatta.

It had a lot of sentimental value, but it ended up going for peanuts.

❑ A *mon* was the smallest unit of monetary value in the Edo era. Originally this expression was written with the character for "foot" 足 (which is also the counter used for pairs of shoes), as in Edo Japan you could buy two pairs of rush sandals for three *mon*. Thereafter the character for "bundle" was used and the expression took on its present meaning.

日常茶飯 *nichijō-sahan*
everyday tea and rice
an everyday occurrence (affair), a daily (common, commonplace, ordinary) occurrence, a common or garden-variety event, no big deal, ten a penny

---

● 今の高校生にとっては、こんなことは日常茶飯だよ。知らないのは親ばかりさ。

Ima no kōkō-sei ni totte wa, konna koto wa nichijō-sahan da yo. Shiranai no wa oya bakari sa.

For today's high-school students something like this is no big deal. The only ones who don't know about it are their parents.

● この程度の事故は、このカーブじゃ日常茶飯事なんですよ。

Kono teido no jiko wa, kono kābu ja nichijō-sahan-ji nan desu yo.

Accidents like that are ten a penny on this corner.

❑ Literally 日常茶飯 means "everyday tea and rice"; the expression is usually followed by the character 事, in which case the meaning is "an everyday occurrence." The character for rice 飯 is also used in the expression 朝飯前 (*asameshi-mae*), which literally means "before breakfast," and is used to refer to something that is easy to do, e.g., 俺ならこんな仕事は朝飯前だ (*Ore nara konna shigoto wa asameshi-mae da*; "A job like that I could do with my eyes closed"). A synonymous expression is お茶の子さいさい (*ocha no ko saisai*). お茶の子 is a small Japanese sweet eaten when drinking green tea, and might be suitably translated as "a piece of cake," as in the following example:

● 任しといて下さい。お茶の子さいさいです。

Makashitoite kudasai. Ocha no ko saisai desu.

Leave it to me. It's a piece of cake.

日曜大工 *nichiyō-daiku*
Sunday carpenter
a DIY fanatic, a do-it-yourself fanatic

● クロも大きくなってきたから、今度の休みにはお父さんが日曜大工で犬小屋を作ってやろう。

Kuro mo ōkiku natte kita kara, kondo no yasumi ni wa otōsan ga nichiyō-daiku de inugoya o tsukutte yarō.

Blackie's now got to be quite a big dog, so Daddy's going to make him a nice kennel, come Sunday.

● あの棚は主人の日曜大工の作品で、ちょっと格好は悪いけど、便利で重宝してるのよ。

Ano tana wa shujin no nichiyō-daiku no sakuhin de, chotto kakkō wa warui kedo, benri de chōhō shite 'ru no yo.

Those shelves are ones my husband knocked up himself. They look a bit naff (ugly), but they come in handy and I couldn't do without them.

日進月歩 *nisshin-geppo*

progress by days and months

steady advance, rapid progress; 〜する to advance by leaps and bounds, to make rapid progress

- パソコンは日進月歩の業界だから、新製品も半年も経つと安く買えるよ。

Pasokon wa nisshin-geppo no gyōkai da kara, shin-seihin mo hantoshi mo tatsu to yasuku kaeru yo.

Advancements in personal computers are happening so fast that new products are discounted after only six months on the market.

- 医療技術は日進月歩しているけれど、患者の心のケアの方はあまり進んでいない。

Iryō-gijutsu wa nisshin-geppo shite iru keredo, kanja no kokoro no kea no hō wa amari susunde inai.

Although medical technology is advancing by leaps and bounds, there has been very little progress in dealing with patients' spiritual well-being.

二人三脚 *ninin-sankyaku*

two people, three legs

a three-legged race, cooperating with singleness of purpose, working together to achieve the same goal

- 小学校の運動会というと、二人三脚とスプーンレースを思い出すなあ。

Shōgakkō no undō-kai to iu to, ninin-sankyaku to supūn-rēsu o omoidasu nā.

Talking of elementary school sports days reminds me of three-legged races and egg-and-spoon contests.

• 今日からは新郎新婦力を合わせて、仲良く二人三脚の人生
をお送り下さい。

*Kyō kara wa shinrō-shinpu chikara o awasete, naka-yoku
ninin-sankyaku no jinsei o ookuri kudasai.*

To the bride and groom I say, please join forces to live in
happy harmony from this day on.

女人禁制 *nyonin-kinsei*

no females allowed

off limits to women, no admittance to women, out-of-
bounds to women

• 昔、高野山は女人禁制だったから、女性は室生寺に参りま
した。室生寺が女人高野と呼ばれるのは、そのためです。

*Mukashi, Kōya-san wa nyonin-kinsei datta kara, josei wa
Murōji ni mairimashita. Murōji ga Nyonin Kōya to yobareru
no wa, sono tame desu.*

In the old days Mount Kōya was strictly out-of-bounds to
women, who instead went to pray at Murō-ji. For that reason
Murō-ji is known as "the women's Mount Kōya."

❏ 高野山 (Kōya-san) is a mountain temple in Wakayama Pre-
fecture, famous as a place of pilgrimage. Long ago only men
were able to visit it, and women were forced to seek spiritual
salvation elsewhere. Murō-ji is a temple in Nara.

• 女人禁制だった山が多いのは、山の神様が女性だと考えら
れていたかららしい。

*Nyonin-kinsei datta yama ga ōi no wa, yama no kamisama ga
josei da to kangaerarete ita kara rashii.*

So many mountains used to be off limits to women because it
was thought the mountain god was a goddess.

• 現在でも土俵は女人禁制で、文部大臣ですら女性は土俵に
は上がれません。

Genzai de mo dohyō wa nyonin-kinsei de, monbu-daijin de sura josei wa dohyō ni wa agaremasen.

Even today women are not allowed to set foot inside the sumo wrestling ring, even if they happen to be the Minister of Education.

❑ At the end of every sumo competition, the champion wrestler is presented with prizes given by various organizations such as foreign embassies, companies, and even the Japanese Education Ministry. In the early 1990s two successive Ministers of Education were women (Mayumi Moriyama and Ryoko Akamatsu). They should have presented the prizes but were prevented from doing so by the sumo authorities, who would not allow them to sully the sacred soil of the sumo ring (where the prize-giving ceremony always takes place). In their place a male underling was sent along from the ministry to hand over the awards instead. Even though this caused a storm of publicity at the time, nothing has changed, and the sumo ring is still a distinctly all-male preserve.

Some older men use the expression 山の神 (*yama no kami*; "the god of the mountain") to refer to their wife (a British equivalent might be "She who must be obeyed"). Perhaps the reason for this is that the said deity was in fact a goddess and not a god, and one with a fearsome reputation for wild pangs of jealousy and anger if any woman should dare to encroach on her domain.

年功序列 *nenkō-joretsu*

years of long service (determine one's) rank
seniority; the seniority system where rank and position are determined by age and the number of years spent working in the company

---

• 日本の雇用制度の特徴と言われてきた終身雇用と年功序列は、いまや崩れつつある。

*Nihon no koyō-seido no tokuchō to iwarete kita shūshin-koyō
to nenkō-joretsu wa, imaya kuzuretsutsu aru.*

Lifetime employment and promotion based on seniority, both
said to be distinctive features of Japan's system of employment, are in the process of disappearing.

● 給与も出世も年功序列で決まるのが当然と思っていたサラ
リーマンは、能力給の導入に戸惑っている。

*Kyūyo mo shusse mo nenkō-joretsu de kimaru no ga tōzen to
omotte ita sararīman wa, nōryoku-kyū no dōnyū ni tomadotte
iru.*

To white-collar workers used to salary and promotion being
determined by the number of years of service, the introduc-
tion of salary levels based on ability is causing bewilder-
ment.

● いくら年功序列でも、あんなトロイ人が課長じゃ、我々は
はっきり言って迷惑ですよ。

*Ikura nenkō-joretsu de mo, anna toroi hito ga kachō ja, ware-
ware wa hakkiri itte meiwaku desu yo.*

I don't care how long he's been with the company; with a sec-
tion chief as stupid as that our life's being made simply impossible.

年齢不詳 *nenrei-fushō*
age unknown
of uncertain age; it's impossible to tell one's age

● 女優には若いんだか老けてるのか分からない人が多いけど、
中でもこの人は年齢不詳だね。

*Joyū ni wa wakai n' da ka fukete 'ru no ka wakaranai hito ga
ōi kedo, naka de mo kono hito wa nenrei-fushō da ne.*

With many actresses you can't tell if they're young or old, but
with her it's simply impossible to guess her age.

- うちの母はまだ20代の体形で、白髪も全然ないから、人からよく年齢不詳だと言われる。

Uchi no haha wa mada nijū-dai no taikei de, shiraga mo zenzen nai kara, hito kara yoku nenrei-fushō da to iwareru.

My mother's got the body of a woman in her twenties and doesn't have a grey hair on her head, so people always say it's impossible to tell her age.

売名行為 *baimei-kōi*
name-selling activity
self-advertisement; a publicity stunt; publicity-seeking

- 彼女は「女優の売名行為だ」という陰口にも負けず、ボランティア活動を続けている。

Kanojo wa "Joyū no baimei-kōi da" to iu kageguchi ni mo makezu, borantia-katsudō o tsuzukete iru.

The actress didn't let snide remarks about it all being a publicity stunt prevent her from continuing her volunteer work.

- 誠意があるか単なる売名行為かは、見る目のある人にはすぐわかってしまうさ。

Seii ga aru ka tannaru baimei-kōi ka wa, miru me no aru hito ni wa sugu wakatte shimau sa.

Anyone with half an eye can tell in an instant whether something is meant sincerely or is only done for publicity.

薄利多売 *hakuri-tabai*
(to make) a thin (small) profit and sell a lot
narrow margin and high turnover

- 当店では薄利多売をモットーに、少しでも良い品をお求めやすいお値段で、ご提供いたしております。

Tōten de wa hakuri-tabai o mottō ni, sukoshi de mo yoi shina o omotomeyasui onedan de, goteikyō itashite orimasu.

The motto at our shop is a narrow margin with high turnover; we endeavor to supply good products at reasonable prices.

● 薄利多売の代表は、何と言ってもディスカウントストアなどの量販店でしょうね。

Hakuri-tabai no daihyō wa, nanto itte mo disukaunto-sutoa nado no ryōhanten deshō ne.

No matter how you look at it, the most representative example of narrow-margin high-turnover selling is the large-volume discount store.

馬耳東風 *baji-tōfū*

the east wind (blowing in) a horse's ear
utter indifference

● 俺は全身全霊をこめて話をした積もりだけど、あいつには馬耳東風だった。

Ore wa zenshin-zenrei o komete hanashi o shita tsumori da kedo, aitsu ni wa baji-tōfū datta.

I put body and soul into telling him all about it, but it seemed to go in one ear and out the other.

● 聞いていないのか、聞いていても馬耳東風なのか、分からないんだ。

Kiite inai no ka, kiite ite mo baji-tōfū na no ka, wakaranai n' da.

I don't know whether he simply didn't hear or whether he heard and just couldn't care less.

→ In Japanese there are several idioms expressing the idea of giving something of value to someone who does not appreciate its worth. One of these 馬の耳に念仏 (*Uma no mimi ni nenbutsu*; "A Buddhist prayer in a horse's ear") is similar to 馬耳東風 (both having the characters for "horse's ear" in common), so care should be taken not to confuse the two expressions. Two further idioms with a similar meaning are 猫に小判 (*Neko ni koban*; "Giving gold coins to a cat") and 豚に真珠 (*Buta ni shinju*; "Casting pearls before swine"). The difference between 馬耳東風 and 馬の耳に念仏 on the one hand and 猫に小判 and 豚に真珠 on the other is that the former can only be used when something intangible is concerned, e.g., advice. The latter can be used for both tangible and intangible things.

❑ The east wind 東風 here refers to the warm wind heralding the arrival of spring, usually called the *harukaze* 春風. The origin of this four-character compound dates from a poem written in the Tang dynasty in ancient China by the poet Rihaku 李白. Here is a free and easy translation of his poem: "After suffering the hardships of the long cold winter, people rejoice at the arrival of the warm winds of spring, but our joy is not shared by the horses of the field." Maybe the horses knew something Rihaku didn't: spring may mean warm winds and pretty flowers for poets, but it also means back-breaking work for farmers and their work animals.

八方美人 *happō-bijin*
an eight-directions beauty
somebody who tries to please everyone (be everybody's friend)

• 彼女は八方美人だからね、誰にどう言えばいいかよく心得てるよ。

Kanojo wa happō-bijin da kara ne, dare ni dō ieba ii ka yoku kokoroete 'ru yo.

She tries to keep on everyone's good side, and is perfectly aware of what to say and when.

• あの八方美人め！　みんなにいい顔しやがって。

Ano happō-bijin-me! Minna ni ii kao shiyagatte.

That flunkey really pisses me off! There's no end to his apple
  polishing.

● 政府の福祉政策は八方美人的で、結局誰も満足していない。

*Seifu no fukushi-seisaku wa happō-bijin-teki de, kekkyoku dare
mo manzoku shite inai.*

The government's welfare policy tries to be all things to all
  people, so it ends up satisfying no one.

波瀾万丈 *haran-banjō*

small waves and big waves rise 10,000 feet

eventful, stormy, full of ups and downs, checkered

● 波瀾万丈の人生でしたが、何も後悔はしていません。

*Haran-banjō no jinsei deshita ga, nani mo kōkai wa shite
imasen.*

I've led a checkered life, but I regret nothing.

● 祖父の一生はまさに波瀾万丈で、僕に文才があれば、小説
  に書きたいくらいだ。

*Sofu no isshō wa masa ni haran-banjō de, boku ni bunsai ga
areba, shōsetsu ni kakitai kurai da.*

Granddad's life was full of incident, and if I had any talent as a
  writer, I'd write a novel about it.

罵詈雑言 *bari-zōgon*

abusive language, rude words

abusive language, cursing and swearing, insults; 〜を
浴びせる (*abiseru*) to shower someone with abuse; to
call someone names (every name in the book)

● 酒の席とはいえ、罵詈雑言を浴びせられて、黙っているわ
  けにはいかなかったんだ。

Sake no seki to wa ie, bari-zōgon o abiserarete, damatte iru wake ni wa ikanakatta n' da.

Even considering that everyone had had a few drinks, I just couldn't sit there after being showered with abuse like that.

● 日本語より英語のほうが罵詈雑言の種類は多いような気がするけど、どう。

Nihongo yori eigo no hō ga bari-zōgon no shurui wa ōi yō na ki ga suru kedo, dō.

I've got a sneaky feeling there are more ways of insulting someone in English than in Japanese. What do you think?

● 社長は総会屋たちの浴びせかける罵詈雑言にじっと耐えていた。

Shachō wa sōkaiya-tachi no abisekakeru bari-zōgon ni jitto taete ita.

The president sat there stoically while the hoodlums at the shareholders meeting rained down invective on him .

万国共通 *bankoku-kyōtsū*
ten thousand countries in common
universal, the same everywhere

● 笑顔は万国共通の挨拶ですね。

Egao wa bankoku-kyōtsū no aisatsu desu ne.

A smile is a universal greeting the world over.

● 地球の環境問題は、万国共通の課題だろう。

Chikyū no kankyō-mondai wa, bankoku-kyōtsū no kadai darō.

The earth's environmental problems are of concern to all people everywhere.

半信半疑 *hanshin-hangi*

half believing, half doubting

incredulous, doubtful, dubious, somewhat suspicious

• 自分の目が信じられず、半信半疑で銀行へ行ったが、本当に当たりくじだった。

Jibun no me ga shinjirarezu, hanshin-hangi de ginkō e itta ga, hontō ni atari-kuji datta.

I couldn't believe my eyes and went to the bank thinking it couldn't be true, but I had really won the lottery.

• すっかりあきらめていたので、合格の知らせが着いてもまだ半信半疑だった。

Sukkari akiramete ita no de, gōkaku no shirase ga tsuite mo mada hanshin-hangi datta.

I had given up all hope, so when news of my exam success reached me, I couldn't believe it was true.

半身不随 *hanshin-fuzui*

half one's body does not obey

partial paralysis, paralyzed on one side (of one's body)

• お隣りのおじいちゃんは、去年の冬脳梗塞で倒れて以来、半身不随で寝たきりです。

Otonari no ojī-chan wa, kyonen no fuyu nō-kōsoku de taorete irai, hanshin-fuzui de neta kiri desu.

The old guy living next door has been bedridden with partial paralysis since he had a stroke last winter.

• わが国の経済は、いまや半身不随の病人に例えられるほど、行き詰まっている。

Wagakuni no keizai wa, imaya hanshin-fuzui no byōnin ni tatoe-rareru hodo, ikizumatte iru.

Our nation's economy can be compared to a partial paralyzed patient: we're stuck and we can't move.

被害妄想 *higai-mōsō*

injury delusions

a persecution complex, paranoia

• 会社が彼を首にしようとして電話を盗聴してるなんて、完全な被害妄想だよ。

Kaisha ga kare o kubi ni shiyō to shite denwa o tōchō shite 'ru nante, kanzen na higai-mōsō da yo.

He's completely paranoid, convinced the company's bugged his phone and is out to sack him.

• あの人の場合、被害妄想と誇大妄想が一緒になっていて、自分は素晴らしく能力があるのに、回りの人たちに妬まれて邪魔されていると思ってるんだ。

Ano hito no bāi, higai-mōsō to kodai-mōsō ga issho ni natte ite, jibun wa subarashiku nōryoku ga aru no ni, mawari no hitotachi ni netamarete jama sarete iru to omotte 'ru n' da.

That guy not only has a persecution complex but delusions of grandeur, too. He's convinced he's brilliantly talented but is being held back by people around him who are jealous of his abilities.

美辞麗句 *biji-reiku*

beautiful language, charming phrases

pretty words, flowery language, highfalutin phrases, purple prose

---

• 内容のお粗末さを美辞麗句でごまかそうとしているのが見え見えさ。

Naiyō no osomatsusa o biji-reiku de gomakasō to shite iru no ga miemie sa.

It's as clear as day that they're trying to cover up for the lack of content by using flowery language.

● 美辞麗句を連ねてあるが、要するに断りの返事だよ。

Biji-reiku o tsuranete aru ga, yōsuru ni kotowari no henji da yo.

They've strung together lots of highfalutin phrases, but what they're basically saying is the answer's no.

百発百中 *hyappatsu-hyakuchū*

one hundred shots, one hundred in the center

hitting the bull's-eye every time, hitting the mark ten times out of ten, always (bang) on target, 100% accurate

---

● この局の天気予報はこのところ百発百中だから、今日は傘を持って行った方がいいよ。

Kono kyoku no tenki-yohō wa kono tokoro hyappatsu-hyaku-chū da kara, kyō wa kasa o motte itta hō ga ii yo.

This channel's weather forecasts have been 100% accurate recently, so you'd better take an umbrella with you today.

● 長島さんの動物的なカンは、百発百中とは行かないまでも、かなりよく当たるらしい。

Nagashima-san no dōbutsu-teki na kan wa, hyappatsu-hyaku-chū to wa ikanai made mo, kanari yoku ataru rashii.

Mr. Nagashima's animal instinct is not quite infallible, but he gets things right pretty often.

● 百発百中は難しいけど、十のうち八つくらいは予想が当たる。

Hyappatsu-hyakuchū wa muzukashii kedo, jū no uchi yattsu kurai wa yosō ga ataru.

Getting ten out of ten is not easy, but I can usually get about eight out of ten right.

疲労困憊 *hirō-konpai*

tiredness and exhaustion

〜する to be totally exhausted, knackered, done in, beat, worn out, dog-tired

---

• 麻雀で疲労困憊だなんて、誰も同情しないよ。

Mājan de hirō-konpai da nante, dare mo dōjō shinai yo.

Exhausted from playing mahjong? You're not going to get much sympathy for that.

• 徹夜が二日も続いたから、みんな疲労困憊している様子だ。

Tetsuya ga futsuka mo tsuzuita kara, minna hirō-konpai shite iru yōsu da.

We've been up for the last two nights without a wink of sleep, and everybody's dog-tired.

• 今思えば当時は連日の残業で、心身ともに疲労困憊していたんだなあ。

Ima omoeba tōji wa renjitsu no zangyō de, shinshin tomo ni hirō-konpai shite ita n' da nā.

Now that I think about it, what with overtime every night, we were just downright exhausted, both mentally and physically.

品行方正 *hinkō-hōsei*

exemplary behavior

exemplary behavior, good (irreproachable) conduct, high morals, upstanding (moral) character

---

• あまりに品行方正なので、とんでもない裏があるんじゃないかとかえって疑ってしまうよ。

Amari ni hinkō-hōsei na no de, tondemonai ura ga aru n' ja nai ka to kaette utagatte shimau yo.

He is a man of such upstanding morals, you actually end up suspecting he must have some awful skeletons in the cupboard (closet).

● 彼は品行方正で、女にも金にも悪い噂など聞いたことがない。

Kare wa hinkō-hōsei de, onna ni mo kane ni mo warui uwasa nado kiita koto ga nai.

He is a man of unimpeachable morals. I have never heard the slightest rumor of dalliances or financial irregularities.

風光明媚 *fūkō-meibi*
the scenery is clear and beautiful
beautiful scenery, picturesque

● こんな風光明媚なところで、老後をすごしたいものだね。

Konna fūkō-meibi na tokoro de, rōgo o sugoshitai mono da ne.

I would love to spend my retirement in a place as picturesque as this.

● 昔は風光明媚だったこの海岸も、すっかり観光化して汚れてしまったよ。

Mukashi wa fūkō-meibi datta kono kaigan mo, sukkari kankō-ka shite yogorete shimatta yo.

In the old days this beach used to be so beautiful, but now it's been totally spoilt by tourism.

不倶戴天 *fugu-taiten*
cannot bear (carry) the same sky
irreconcilable (foes)

● あいつは俺のいわば不倶戴天の敵なんだ。

Aitsu wa ore no iwaba fugu-taiten no teki nan da.

That guy's what you might call a mortal enemy.

● 青山さんと赤坂さんは、昔から不倶戴天の間柄だ。

Aoyama-san to Akasaka-san wa, mukashi kara fugu-taiten no aidagara da.

Aoyama and Akasaka have been at each other's throats for as long as I can remember.

不言実行 *fugen-jikkō*

silent action

action speaks louder than words; 〜の人 a quiet man of action

● 私は古い人間かもしれないが、不言実行が好きだ。

Watashi wa furui ningen ka mo shirenai ga, fugen-jikkō ga suki da.

I may be old-fashioned, but I like getting things done without a lot of fuss.

● 不言実行は、ともすれば不言不実行になってしまうおそれがあるよ。

Fugen-jikkō wa, tomosureba fugen-fujikkō ni natte shimau osore ga aru yo.

If you are not careful, getting things done without a lot of fuss can end up meaning getting nothing done at all.

❑ Japanese who are articulate and good at expressing their ideas are not always popular. Getting on with things without talking about them (不言実行) is seen as a virtue. Many people have commented on how the Japanese prefer intuitive ways of communicating over verbal ones. There is "the art of the belly" (腹芸 *haragei*; the intuitive way of guessing what the other means), and "the transferal of one's true intent from one heart to another" (以心伝心 *ishin-denshin*). This is not altogether a wholly Japanese phenomenon; after all, we do say in

English "Actions speak louder than words," and a fair number of Hollywood's biggest male stars are more famous for their action-packed performances than their mastery of the English language. The saying "Silence is golden" exists in both languages (the Japanese being 沈黙は金, *chinmoku wa kin*).

夫唱婦随 *fushō-fuzui*
the husband speaks, the wife obeys
a loving couple (where the wife is happy to play second fiddle to her husband)

- いまどき夫唱婦随が理想だなんて言ってるから、結婚相手が見つからないんじゃないの。

Imadoki fushō-fuzui ga risō da nante itte 'ru kara, kekkon-aite ga mitsukaranai n' ja nai no.

It's precisely because you say you're looking for a woman to be at your beck and call that you can't find anyone to marry you!

- このごろでは夫唱婦随ならぬ婦唱夫随の家庭も多いんじゃないでしょうか。

Konogoro de wa fushō-fuzui naranu fushō-fuzui no katei mo ōi n' ja nai deshō ka.

These days there seem to be a good many families in which the wife not only washes her husband's pants but wears them, too.

不偏不党 *fuhen-futō*
without bias and free from party affiliation
impartial, neutral, non-partisan, fair, unbiased, independent

• 公務員は政治的には不偏不党が建前だ。

Kōmu-in wa seiji-teki ni wa fuhen-futō ga tatemae da.

Civil servants are supposed to be free of political bias.

• 長田教授は学閥に属さないで不偏不党の、いわば一匹狼だ。

Nagata-kyōju wa gakubatsu ni zokusanai de fuhen-futō no, iwaba ippiki-ōkami da.

Professor Nagata is what you might call a lone wolf, not aligning himself with any academic clique.

不眠不休 *fumin-fukyū*
without sleep, without rest
(to work hard) with no sleep or rest, day and night, twenty-four hours a day, non-stop, round-the-clock

---

• 不眠不休の勤務が続いて、過労死がひと事とは思えなくなった。

Fumin-fukyū no kinmu ga tsuzuite, karō-shi ga hitogoto to wa omoenaku natta.

Since I've been working flat out for quite a while, it's beginning to dawn on me that dying from overwork isn't just something that happens to other people.

• 救援隊の不眠不休の活動のおかげで、多くの生存者が救出された。

Kyūen-tai no fumin-fukyū no katsudō no okage de, ōku no seizon-sha ga kyūshutsu sareta.

Many survivors were rescued thanks to the round-the-clock efforts of the emergency services.

• 医師は不眠不休で、患者の容態を見守った。

Ishi wa fumin-fukyū de, kanja no yōtai o mimamotta.

The doctor maintained a round-the-clock vigil, closely monitoring the patient's condition.

不要不急 *fuyō-fukyū*

unnecessary and not urgent

not pressing, not vital

● 回線が混雑していますので、不要不急の電話は避けて下さい。

Kaisen ga konzatsu shite imasu no de, fuyō-fukyū no denwa wa sakete kudasai.

The phone lines are very busy so please don't make a call unless it is really urgent.

● 午後から大雪になる見込みですから、不要不急の用事の場合は出かけないほうがいいでしょう。

Gogo kara ōyuki ni naru mikomi desu kara, fuyō-fukyū no yōji no bāi wa dekakenai hō ga ii deshō.

The outlook is for heavy snow from the afternoon, so unless you have urgent business, you'd be better off staying in.

暴飲暴食 *bōin-bōshoku*

violent drinking, violent eating

make a pig of oneself, overeat and overdrink, stuff oneself stupid with food and drink

---

● 暴飲暴食はやめなさい。「腹も身の内」だよ。

Bōin-bōshoku wa yamenasai. "Hara mo mi no uchi" da yo.

Stop making such a pig of yourself. Remember, you are what you eat.

❑ 腹も身の内 (*hara mo mi no uchi*) is a Japanese saying with no direct equivalent in English. Paraphrased it means "Your stomach is part of your body too, you know, so you'd better take care of it."

- お前みたいに毎日暴飲暴食を続けてると、いまに胃をこわすよ。

Omae mitai ni mainichi bōin-bōshoku o tsuzukete 'ru to, ima ni i o kowasu yo.

If you go on stuffing yourself full of food and drink, you'll ruin your stomach.

傍若無人 *bōjaku-bujin*

as if there were no one around (in old Japanese 若 means "as if")

arrogance, audacity, insolence, defiance, recklessness

- 彼の傍若無人な自己主張には、腹が立つより先に呆れてしまう。

Kare no bōjaku-bujin na jiko-shuchō ni wa, hara ga tatsu yori saki ni akirete shimau.

I'm not so much angry at his outrageous selfishness as simply amazed.

- あんな傍若無人のふるまいが通るのも、社長の娘と結婚してるからだ。

Anna bōjaku-bujin no furumai ga tōru no mo, shachō no musume to kekkon shite 'ru kara da.

The reason he can get away with such outrageous behavior is that he's married to the boss's daughter.

本末転倒 *honmatsu-tentō*

the beginning and the end reversed

getting one's priorities all wrong (mixed up); putting the cart before the horse

---

• 教師が学生から注意されるなんて、本末転倒じゃないか。
情けない。

*Kyōshi ga gakusei kara chūi sareru nante, honmatsu-tentō ja
nai ka. Nasakenai.*

When the students start correcting their teachers, you know
something is drastically wrong. A pretty sad situation if you
ask me.

• 節税のために借金するなんて本末転倒だと思うけどなあ。

*Setsuzei no tame ni shakkin suru nante honmatsu-tentō da to
omou kedo nā.*

Taking out a loan just to reduce your taxes makes me think
you've got your priorities all wrong.

満員電車 *man'in-densha*
a full-of-people train
a jam-packed train

• 毎日満員電車に乗って通勤するのが嫌で、田舎にUターン
したんだ。

*Mainichi man'in-densha ni notte tsūkin suru no ga iya de,
inaka ni yūtān shita n' da.*

I couldn't stand the daily commute on a packed train, so I
moved back to my hometown.

• 今朝、満員電車の中で、痴漢と間違えられて、思いっきり
足踏まれた。

*Kesa, man'in-densha no naka de, chikan to machigaerarete,
omoikkiri ashi fumareta.*

This morning, a woman on the rush-hour train thought I was
molesting her and trod on my foot with all her might.

❑ 痴漢 (*chikan*) is a sexual molester (invariably a man) who
often harasses women on the trains (hoping, one presumes, his

victims will be unable to tell who their tormentor is and be unable to defend themselves, as the trains are so packed it is virtually impossible to move).

三日天下 *mikka-tenka*

three days' reign

a short-lived reign, a very brief reign, to be in power for a very short time

---

• 権力闘争の末、やっと首相になったが、女性問題のスキャンダルで三日天下に終わった。

Kenryoku-tōsō no sue, yatto shushō ni natta ga, josei-mondai no sukyandaru de mikka-tenka ni owatta.

At the end of a power struggle he at last became prime minister, but his premiership was short-lived after he was caught having a extramarital affair.

• 重役会の造反で、新社長は退任に追込まれ、三日天下だった。

Jūyaku-kai no zōhan de, shin-shachō wa tainin ni oikomare, mikka-tenka datta.

The new president got caught up in a revolt by the board of directors and soon found himself out of a job (ousted from office).

❏ The origin of this expression dates from the Sengoku era, when Akechi Mitsuhide made a surprise attack on Oda Nobunaga at Honnō-ji in Kyoto and wrested power from him, only to lose it to Toyotomi Hideyoshi almost immediately.

三日坊主 *mikka-bōzu*

a three-day priest

someone who starts something only to give it up at once, someone with no staying power, (he) won't keep it up for long, (he) never sticks to anything for very long, it won't last

---

● 今年も日記帳を買ったが、三日坊主だからいつまで続くことやら。

Kotoshi mo nikki-chō o katta ga, mikka-bōzu da kara itsu made tsuzuku koto yara.

I bought a diary again this year, but with my usual lack of stick-to-itiveness, who knows how long I'll keep it up.

● 姉のダイエットは、今回も三日坊主に終わった。

Ane no daietto wa, konkai mo mikka-bōzu ni owatta.

My big sister went on a diet again, but as usual she soon gave it up.

● 結果は三日坊主だったけど、一度はやる気になっただけいいじゃないか。

Kekka wa mikka-bōzu datta kedo, ichido wa yaru-ki ni natta dake ii ja nai ka.

It didn't last very long, but at least you had the gumption to give it a try.

→ Here "three days" simply means "a short period of time," not necessarily 72 hours.

無我夢中 *muga-muchū*

selfless absorption

to lose oneself in, to be totally absorbed (immersed, engrossed, wrapped up) in, to forget oneself

- 当時は無我夢中だったから何とも思わなかったが、今考えるとよくあんなことに耐えられたと我ながら感心する。

Tōji wa muga-muchū datta kara nan to mo omowanakatta ga, ima kangaeru to yoku anna koto ni taerareta to warenagara kanshin suru.

At the time I was totally absorbed in what I was doing so I didn't think much about it, but looking back now, I'm amazed how I managed to get through it all.

- 無我夢中でプラモデル組み立ててるから、今は何を言っても聞こえませんよ。

Muga-muchū de puramoderu kumitatete 'ru kara, ima wa nani o itte mo kikoemasen yo.

He's putting a plastic model together and lost to the world, so he won't hear a word you say.

無芸大食 *mugei-taishoku*
a talentless big eater
someone whose only talent is eating

- お恥ずかしいんですが無芸大食で、カラオケもてんでだめなんですよ、勘弁してください。

Ohazukashii n' desu ga mugei-taishoku de, karaoke mo tende dame nan desu yo, kanben shite kudasai.

I hate to admit it (to be a party-pooper), but all I'm good at is eating. I'm terrible at karaoke, so I'll have to pass on this one.

- 彼が自分は無芸大食だって言うのは、謙遜じゃなくて本当なんだよ。

Kare ga jibun wa mugei-taishoku datte iu no wa, kenson ja nakute hontō nan da yo.

When he says he doesn't have a talent to his name but filling his face, he's not being modest—it's the truth.

無病息災 *mubyō-sokusai*

without sickness, stopping devastation

as fit as a fiddle, hale and hearty, in sound (good) health

• お金よりも地位よりも、無病息災が何よりですね。

Okane yori mo chii yori mo, mubyō-sokusai ga nani yori desu ne.

Health and fitness are what's important, not money and position.

• 初詣で、今年一年の家族の無病息災を祈ってきた。

Hatsumōde de, kotoshi ichinen no kazoku no mubyō-sokusai o inotte kita.

When I visited the shrine at the New Year, I prayed that my family would remain hale and hearty for the coming twelve months.

❏ Everyone wants to be healthy, but many Japanese believe that in middle age it is better to have some minor ailment since then we are more likely to pay closer attention to our physical condition. This idea of one ailment keeping us on our toes, vigilant as to our health, is expressed as 一病息災 (*ichibyō-sokusai*; "One ailment keeps you healthy").

無味乾燥 *mumi-kansō*

tasteless and dry

dull, tasteless, bland, uninteresting, boring, insipid, vapid, prosaic

---

• 今日の主賓のスピーチは、なんとも面白みがなくて無味乾燥だったね。

Kyō no shuhin no supīchi wa, nan to mo omoshiromi ga nakute mumi-kansō datta ne.

The speech by the guest of honor today was not only uninteresting but downright inane.

● 誰が書いたか知らないけど、すいぶんと無味乾燥な挨拶状だ。

Dare ga kaita ka shiranai kedo, zuibun to mumi-kansō na aisatsu-jō da.

I don't know who wrote this, but it's a pretty insipid greeting card.

滅私奉公 *messhi-hōkō*
self-destruction, public service
selfless service for the common good, to put the country's needs before one's own

---

● 今でもお役所では滅私奉公が要求されるみたいですね。

Ima de mo oyakusho de wa messhi-hōkō ga yōkyū sareru mitai desu ne.

Even today it seems that government offices demand that you sacrifice your personal life to your work.

● 東京にいた頃の僕は、典型的な滅私奉公の猛烈社員だったものだよ。

Tōkyō ni ita koro no boku wa, tenkei-teki na messhi-hōkō no mōretsu-shain datta mono da yo.

When I was in Tokyo I used to be a typical gung-ho company employee, happy to put the company's needs before my own.

● 高度成長時代の日本のサラリーマンは、滅私奉公の精神で遮二無二働いた。

Kōdo-seichō jidai no nihon no sararīman wa, messhi-hōkō no seishin de shani-muni hataraita.

During the postwar period of high economic growth Japanese

white-collar workers worked themselves to the bone in self-less sacrifice to rebuild the nation's wealth.

猛烈社員 *mōretsu-shain*

a zealous employee

an eager-beaver employee, hard worker, tireless worker, workaholic

---

- 猛烈社員として働いて、やっと管理職になった途端に、リストラの対象にされた。

Mōretsu-shain toshite hataraite, yatto kanri-shoku ni natta totan ni, risutora no taishō ni sareta.

I worked my butt off as an eager-beaver employee, and then the minute I finally get a management position, I'm targeted in the company's restructuring.

- 主人は日曜日も会社へ行くような猛烈社員なので、過労死が心配なんです。

Shujin wa nichiyōbi mo kaisha e iku yō na mōretsu-shain na no de, karōshi ga shinpai nan desu.

My husband's the kind of tireless worker who goes into the office even on Sundays, and I'm worried he's going to work himself to death.

有形無形 *yūkei-mukei*

with shape, without shape

visible and invisible, material and spiritual, concrete and moral, tangible and intangible

---

- 友だちから有形無形の援助をしてもらって、とても助かりました。

Tomodachi kara yūkei-mukei no enjō o shite moratte, totemo tasukarimashita.

I received a great deal of support from my friends, both material and moral, which really helped a lot.

• 彼はよい家柄に生まれたことで、有形無形の恩恵を受けて
いる。

Kare wa yoi iegara ni umareta koto de, yūkei-mukei no onkei o ukete iru.

Being born with a silver spoon in his mouth, he had a headstart in life in innumerable ways, both tangible and intangible.

• 長期にわたって有形無形の圧力をかけられて、ついに屈した。

Chōki ni watatte yūkei-mukei no atsuryoku o kakerarete, tsui ni kusshita.

After a long spell of having all manner of pressure brought to bear on me, I've finally thrown in the towel.

優柔不断 *yūjū-fudan*
indecisive and irresolute
indecision, to be indecisive, to vacillate, to waver, to shilly-shally

---

• 今度の上司は優柔不断で、新しい企画案を出しても取り上
げてもらえないんだよ。

Kondo no jōshi wa yūjū-fudan de, atarashii kikaku-an o dashi-te mo toriagete moraenai n' da yo.

Our new boss is incapable of making a decision. Try putting forward a new planning proposal—it'll never see the light of day.

• いつまでも優柔不断なこと言ってたから、彼女は別の人と
見合いしてさっさと結婚したんじゃないか。

Itsu made mo yūjū-fudan na koto itte 'ta kara, kanojo wa betsu no hito to miai shite sassa to kekkon shita n' ja nai ka.

You never stopped humming and hahing, so she went off and got married to some guy she'd been introduced to by relatives.

誘導尋問 *yūdō-jinmon*
leading interrogation
a leading question

- 女房の誘導尋問にひっかかって、へそくりがばれてしまったよ。

Nyōbō no yūdō-jinmon ni hikkakatte, hesokuri ga barete shimatta yo.

I got caught off guard by a leading question, and my wife found out about the money I'd been squirreling away.

- 母は、私が今誰とつきあってるのか知りたくて、誘導尋問してくるんだけど、その手にはのらないわ。

Haha wa, watashi ga ima dare to tsukiatte 'ru no ka shiritakute, yūdō-jinmon shite kuru n' da kedo, sono te ni wa noranai wa.

My mother always wants to know who I'm going out with and keeps asking leading questions, but I'm not falling for that one.

有名無実 *yūmei-mujitsu*
the name exists, but the reality doesn't
nominal, titular, in name alone, famous (but unjustly so)

- 名医だという話だったけど、あの先生の評判は有名無実だよ。

Meii da to iu hanashi datta kedo, ano sensei no hyōban wa yūmei-mujitsu da yo.

He was supposed to be an excellent doctor, but his reputation turned out to be without any foundation in fact.

- あんな有名無実なヒヤリングは、いくらやっても無駄だ。

Anna yūmei-mujitsu na hiyaringu wa, ikura yatte mo muda da.

There's no use holding any more meaningless "hearings" like that.

• 社長と言っても、僕の肩書は有名無実なんですよ。

Shachō to itte mo, boku no katagaki wa yūmei-mujitsu nan desu yo.

I am CEO in name only.

勇猛果敢 *yūmō-kakan*

very brave and decisive

dauntless courage and decisiveness

• 強者ぞろいの中でも、彼は抜きんでて勇猛果敢だった。

Tsuwamono zoroi no naka de mo, kare wa nukinde 'te yūmō-kakan datta.

Even in the midst of such mighty men, he stood out as being the bravest and the boldest of them all.

• 司令官みずから勇猛果敢に戦った。

Shirei-kan mizukara yūmō-kakan ni tatakatta.

With a total disregard for his own safety the commander courageously threw himself into the thick of battle.

行方不明 *yukue-fumei*

whereabouts unclear

to be missing; whereabouts unknown

• 妻が家出して行方不明になってから、もう半年になります。

Tsuma ga iede shite yukue-fumei ni natte kara, mō hantoshi ni narimasu.

It's already been six months now since my wife left home and disappeared.

• 長いこと行方不明だった本が、机の裏から出てきたよ。

Nagai koto yukue-fumei datta hon ga, tsukue no ura kara dete kita yo.

That book that was missing for so long has turned up behind my desk.

❏ When people move house without informing others of their new address, post that is delivered to their former address is returned to the sender stamped 移転先不明 (*itensaki-fumei*; new address unknown). The Japanese for "of no fixed abode" is 住所不定 (*jūsho-futei*), and is now commonly used in reference to the homeless.

油断大敵 *yudan-taiteki*

carelessness is the greatest enemy

danger comes when you least expect it; there is many a slip twixt the cup and the lip; Be very careful! Be on your guard! Watch your step!

• あいつは意外と口が軽いから、うっかりしたことは言えないね。油断大敵だ。

Aitsu wa igai to kuchi ga karui kara, ukkari shita koto wa ienai ne. Yudan-taiteki da.

You wouldn't think it but he's a real chatterbox, so you've got to be careful what you say. A word to the wise.

• やさしいとたかをくくって試験に臨んだのが油断大敵さ、不合格だったよ。

Yasashii to taka o kukutte shiken ni nozonda no ga yudan-taiteki sa, fu-gōkaku datta yo.

I really slipped up big this time. I thought the exam was going to be a cinch, but guess who ended up failing.

用意周到 *yōi-shūtō*

exhaustive preparation

mindfulness, cautiousness, prudence, thoroughgoing
preparation, to be prepared for all eventualities, to be
thoroughly prepared

• 雨靴まで履いて来たとは、ずいぶん用意周到だねえ。

Amagutsu made haite kita to wa, zuibun yōi-shūtō da nē.

He was really well prepared; he had even come wearing his
gumboots (galoshes).

• 用意周到に準備したつもりだったのに、地図を忘れて来ち
ゃったよ。

*Yōi-shūtō ni junbi shita tsumori datta no ni, chizu o wasurete
kichatta yo.*

I thought I'd thought of everything, but then I ended up forget-
ting the map.

• いつ外泊してもいいように、バッグに着替えと洗面用具入
れて歩いてるんですか。用意周到な人と言うべきか、遊び
人と言うべきか……。

*Itsu gaihaku shite mo ii yō ni, baggu ni kigae to senmen-yōgu
irete aruite 'ru n' desu ka. Yōi-shūtō na hito to iu beki ka,
asobinin to iu beki ka ...*

What? She always goes round with a change of clothes and
some toiletries in her bag "just in case"? I don't know
whether to call her well prepared or simply loose.

用意万端 *yōi-bantan*

everything ready

everything is ready and set

• 用意万端整いましたので、会場の方へどうぞ。

Yōi-bantan totonoimashita no de, kaijō no hō e dōzo.

All is set and ready to go, so if you'd just like to make your way to the assembly hall, please.

羊頭狗肉 *yōtō-kuniku*

a sheep's head, but dog meat

cry wine and sell vinegar, make extravagant (and false) claims for a product, false advertising

---

- テレビのコマーシャルとは大違いじゃないの、羊頭狗肉の商法だわ。

Terebi no komāsharu to wa ōchigai ja nai no, yōtō-kuniku no shōhō da wa.

It's nothing like the TV commercial at all. That's blatantly false advertising.

- 面白そうなテーマで、講師の肩書も立派だったのに、全然つまらない羊頭狗肉の講演だった。

Omoshirosō na tēma de, kōshi no katagaki mo rippa datta no ni, zenzen tsumaranai yōtō-kuniku no kōen datta.

The subject looked interesting, and the lecturer had impressive credentials, but it turned out to be a really boring lecture. I felt like I'd been swindled.

立身出世 *risshin-shusse*

going up in the world

success in life, getting ahead, getting on in the world, making a success of yourself, going out into the world and making a name for yourself

---

- 明治時代の日本では、大学さえ出ていれば立身出世の道が開けていた。

Meiji-jidai no nihon de wa, daigaku sae dete ireba risshin-shusse no michi ga hirakete ita.

In Meiji Japan, as long as you had a university education the road to success was assured.

● 立身出世だけが人生の目的じゃないだろう。

Risshin-shusse dake ga jinsei no mokuteki ja nai darō.

Getting ahead in the world isn't the only purpose in life, you know.

● 若くして立身出世しただけに、かなり無理もしたらしいよ。

Wakaku shite risshin-shusse shita dake ni, kanari muri mo shita rashii yo.

He's done well, making a name for himself in the world while still a young man, but it appears to have taken its toll.

流言飛語 *ryūgen-higo*
flowing speech, flying words
wild (unfounded) rumors

● 皆さん、流言飛語に惑わされないでください。

Mina-san, ryūgen-higo ni madowasarenai de kudasai.

Please do not let yourselves be led astray by all the rumors that are flying around.

● 大震災の後、流言飛語が広がり、たくさんの被災者がパニックに陥った。

Dai-shinsai no ato, ryūgen-higo ga hirogari, takusan no hisai-sha ga panikku ni ochiitta.

Wild rumors started to spread after the big earthquake, and many of the victims were thrown into panic.

● 無責任な流言飛語が引き金になって、悲惨な事件が起きてしまった。

Mu-sekinin na ryūgen-higo ga hikigane ni natte, hisan na jiken ga okite shimatta.

Irresponsible rumors were the trigger that led to a tragic event.

● 政府は流言飛語を打ち消そうと躍起になっているが、うまくいかない。

Seifu wa ryūgen-higo o uchikesō to yakki ni natte iru ga, umaku ikanai.

The government is doing its utmost to quash the wild rumors but without much success.

竜頭蛇尾 *ryūtō-dabi*

a dragon's head, a snake's tail

a fast start and a slow finish, ending in an anti-climax, dwindling out; petering out, fizzling out, a tame ending, to start well but fade badly, to fail miserably after a good start

---

● 社運を懸けたプロジェクトのはずだったけど、竜頭蛇尾に終わってしまった。

Shaun o kaketa purojekuto no hazu datta kedo, ryūtō-dabi ni owatte shimatta.

It was supposed to be the project that decided the company's future, but it ended not with a bang but a whimper.

● この本、初めのほうはおもしろかったけど結末は竜頭蛇尾で、読んで損したよ。

Kono hon, hajime no hō wa omoshirokatta kedo ketsumatsu wa ryūtō-dabi de, yonde son shita yo.

The book started strong but petered out at the end. It was a waste of my time.

良妻賢母 *ryōsai-kenbo*

a good wife and wise mother
a model wife and mother

• 本校は創立以来、良妻賢母教育をその柱としております。

Honkō wa sōritsu irai, ryōsai-kenbo-kyōiku o sono hashira to shite orimasu.

Since the school's foundation its ethos has been to educate young girls to become model wives and mothers.

• 良妻賢母の鑑のようだったお隣の奥さんが、年下の男の人と駆け落ちしたそうですよ。

Ryōsai-kenbo no kagami no yō datta otonari no oku-san ga, toshishita no otoko no hito to kakeochi shita sō desu yo.

Our neighbor's wife seemed to be the perfect wife and mother, but now I hear she's run off with a younger man.

臨機応変 *rinki-ōhen*

adapting to circumstances
extemporaneously, impromptu, flexibility, adapting to circumstances as they arise (on an ad hoc basis)

• 二言目には規則、規則って言わないで、もっと臨機応変に考えてもらえませんかね。

Futakoto-me ni wa kisoku, kisoku tte iwanai de, motto rinki-ōhen ni kangaete moraemasen ka ne.

Can't you open your mouth without talking about rules and regulations for once? It'd be nice if we could see a little more flexibility.

• 担当者の臨機応変の対応が望まれる。

Tantō-sha no rinki-ōhen no taiō ga nozomareru.

It is to be hoped that those in charge will show some flexibility in their response.

冷却期間 *reikyaku-kikan*

cooling period
a cooling-off period

● 今は頭に血が上ってるから、何を言ってもだめですよ。冷却期間を置いて、また話しましょう。

Ima wa atama ni chi ga nobotte 'ru kara, nani o itte mo dame desu yo. Reikyaku-kikan o oite, mata hanashimashō.

They're mad as hell right now, so whatever you say it won't do any good. Let's talk to them again after they've cooled down.

● 少しの間会わない、冷却期間があった方がいいと思うんだ。

Sukoshi no aida awanai, reikyaku-kikan ga atta hō ga ii to omou n' da.

Why don't we have a cooling-off period and not see each other for a while?

冷静沈着 *reisei-chinchaku*

cool quietude, calm composure
cool; calm and collected; as cool as a cucumber

● あわや暗殺されるところだったのに、大統領の態度は驚くほど冷静沈着だった。

Awaya ansatsu sareru tokoro datta no ni, daitōryō no taido wa odoroku hodo reisei-chinchaku datta.

Although he had just escaped assassination by a hair's breadth, the president astonished everyone with his cool, calm composure.

• いざとなると、避難訓練通り冷静沈着に行動するのは無理
だろう。

*Iza to naru to, hinan-kunren dōri reisei-chinchaku ni kōdō
suru no wa muri darō.*

When it comes to the real thing, there's no way everyone's
going to act as calm and collected as they do during a
routine evacuation drill.

連鎖反応 *rensa-hannō*

link chain response
chain reaction

• 一人が辞表を出すと、連鎖反応で次々に辞める人が出てき
た。

*Hitori ga jihyō o dasu to, rensa-hannō de tsugitsugi ni yameru
hito ga dete kita.*

When one guy handed in his resignation, others began to quit
in a chain reaction.

• 笑い声は連鎖反応を起こして、さざなみのように広がって
行った。

*Waraigoe wa rensa-hannō o okoshite, sazanami no yō ni hi-
rogatte itta.*

Her laughter started off a chain reaction and spread like ripples
on a pond.

老若男女 *rōnyaku-nannyo*

the old, the young, men and women
people of all ages and both sexes, men and women of
all ages, everybody (irrespective of age or sex)

• 老若男女のどなたでも、それぞれに楽しめる施設が整った
お宿です。

Rōnyaku-nannyo no donata de mo, sorezore ni tanoshimeru shisetsu ga totonotta oyado desu.

This inn is fully equipped with facilities that can be enjoyed by anyone of any age.

● 広場に集まった人々は、老若男女を問わず盆踊りを楽しんでいた。

Hiroba ni atsumatta hitobito wa, rōnyaku-nannyo o towazu bon-odori o tanoshinde ita.

People of all ages were gathered together in the square enjoying the Bon Festival dance.

和洋折衷 *wayō-setchū*

Japanese and Western mixture

a mix (mixture) of Japanese and Western styles

● この本は英語と日本語が入り交じっているから、和洋折衷ですね。

Kono hon wa eigo to nihongo ga irimajitte iru kara, wayō-setchū desu ne.

This book could be called a mixture of the Japanese with the Western as it contains both English and Japanese.

● 家じゃ畳の部屋にベッドで寝て、ご飯と味噌汁の後でコーヒー飲んで、という和洋折衷で暮らしていますよ。

Uchi ja tatami no heya ni beddo de nete, gohan to misoshiru no ato de kōhī nonde, to iu wayō-setchū de kurashite imasu yo.

At home, life is a mixture of the Japanese and the Western: my bedroom floor's covered in tatami but I sleep in a bed; I eat rice and miso soup, then have a cup of coffee.

● 現代の日本では純日本式の生活をしている人は少数派で、大多数の人は衣食住のすべての面、特に食と住において和洋折衷になっています。

Gendai no nihon de wa jun-nihonshiki no seikatsu o shite iru hito wa shōsū-ha de, dai-tasū no hito wa i-shoku-jū no subete no men, toku ni shoku to jū ni oite wayō-setchū ni natte imasu.

In present-day Japan people living in a purely Japanese way are in the minority. When it comes to food, clothing, and shelter (and especially in food and shelter), most people have adopted a mixture of Japanese and Western styles.

❏ Another four-character compound containing the characters for Japan (和) and the West (洋) is 和魂洋才 (*wakon-yōsai*), which literally means "a Japanese soul with Western learning." In the Meiji era Japan imported Western learning wholesale but at the same time strove to maintain its own cultural identity. Although this four-character compound is rarely used in conversation today, you might well come across it when reading about Japanese history, so it is perhaps worth including in your passive vocabulary.